W9-ADK-503

THE
FREEDOM OF
OBEDIENCE

*THE CHRISTIAN
CHARACTER LIBRARY
aims to help Christians live out
the biblical mandate to
become "salt" and "light" in
our world through the witness
of Christlike character.
In its radical essence, Christian
character is not an accumulation
of personal virtues, nor is it a
lifestyle—it is a life. It is
the life of the risen, living Lord
Jesus who expresses His nature
through us as we surrender our
hearts and lives to Him daily.
As we study His life in the
Scriptures and commune with
Him in prayer, He removes
the veil of our sin-darkened
nature and transforms us
into His own likeness with
ever-increasing glory.
The books in The Christian
Character Library have
been written with the purpose
of encouraging you to model the
character of our Lord Jesus
Christ in a way that bears
fruit in the lives of other
people—through the power of a
life that reflects
"Christ in you, the hope of glory."*

MARTHA THATCHER

T · H · E

FREEDOM OF
OBEDIENCE

CHOOSING THE WAY OF TRUE LIBERATION

NAVPRESS
A MINISTRY OF THE NAVIGATORS
P.O. Box 6000, Colorado Springs, Colorado 80934

The Navigators is an international Christian organization. Jesus Christ gave His followers the Great Commission to go and make disciples (Matthew 28:19). The aim of The Navigators is to help fulfill that commission by multiplying laborers for Christ in every nation.

NavPress is the publishing ministry of The Navigators. NavPress publications are tools to help Christians grow. Although publications alone cannot make disciples or change lives, they can help believers learn biblical discipleship, and apply what they learn to their lives and ministries.

© 1986 by Martha Thatcher
All rights reserved, including translation
Library of Congress Catalog Card Number:
    86-61137
ISBN: 08910-91939

Cover illustration: Gary Kelley

First printing, paperback edition, 1987

Unless otherwise identified, all Scripture quotations in the publication are from the *Holy Bible: New International Version* (NIV). Copyright © 1973, 1978, 1984, International Bible Society. Used by permission of Zondervan Bible Publishers. Other versions quoted are the *Amplified New Testament* (AMP), © The Lockman Foundation 1954, 1958; the *New American Standard Bible* (NASB), © The Lockman Foundation 1960, 1962, 1963, 1968, 1971, 1972, 1973, 1975, 1977; and the *Revised Standard Version of the Bible* (RSV), copyrighted 1946, 1952, © 1971, 1973.

Printed in the United States of America

FOR A FREE CATALOG OF
NAVPRESS BOOKS & BIBLE STUDIES,
CALL TOLL FREE 800-525-7151 (USA)
or 800-263-2664 (CANADA)

Contents

Author

Martha Thatcher and her husband, Brian, are on staff with The Navigators in Ontario, Canada. Martha is a graduate of Barrington College. She and Brian have three children.

Introduction

I had lost all sense of time. Gripped in an unexpected struggle, my mind and body had suspended normal routine while the outcome of my grappling hung in the balance. What had begun as an uneventful—even boring—literature assignment had become for me an issue of crucial significance, an issue of pivotal thinking. Isolated and oblivious in a nook of the college library that winter afternoon, I had a sense that my life was about to turn a corner.

On the desk before me, my book was open to the article I was studying: freedom versus structure. Also before me, two stacks of index cards reminded me that I had a paper to write. An unlikely setting for the birth of a crisis! But there I was, pondering the idea that if freedom is the absence of limitations—as I supposed and read that it is—then structure is that which prevents freedom. Freedom and structure are enemies.

Implications abounded, but the most threatening was the dark thought that as I looked ahead to a structured life, a life in the process of conforming to God's ways, I would know little of freedom. My struggle came down to this: How could knowing and obeying God's truth set me free, as I had read in John 8:32 that it would?

The question left me numb, and I stared out the window. From over the row of century-old pine trees, a jet drew its frothy white stripe across my view. And with that image came a sudden awakening: The jet flew because it conformed to the laws of aerodynamics. Conformity to structure had given birth to the freedom of flight!

For centuries man had sought that freedom. He had made all manner of logical and outrageous devices to leave the ground and glide on the wind. When did his dream become reality? When he understood and submitted to the God-made laws concerning flight. When he did it God's way, man was free to fly.

Freedom and structure are not enemies, but inseparable companions in God's paradoxical truth. The article was expounding a lie. And I was vulnerable to the lie because I had no understanding of how obedience to God could mean freedom. My understanding of biblical obedience itself was fuzzy. Like the wing-makers of old, I tried hard but sooner or later always ended up back where I started. My attempts to obey were well-intentioned and earnest, but usually brought about no lasting change in my life. The Bible courses and studies I took increased my knowledge, but not my intimacy with God.

An earlier shattering incident had brought me face to face with the fact that I was not growing in Christ. That realization had prompted my initial desire to search out what God meant by obedience, and how He meant me to carry it out. I had tried my version of the obedient Christian life. Now, with a new understanding of God's intention, I was ready to do it His way. And taste His freedom.

A life-changing adventure had begun.

1
Loving God: The Essence of Obedience

The agony in the old man's heart issued not from indecision; he had made the decision long ago. This agony was the pain of the price—the high price of commitment. He learned all his lessons in pain, it seemed, but this pain exceeded every other.

Daring no sideward glance at the boy Isaac, Abraham resumed the climb. They had left the servants in a makeshift camp, and in the privacy of their relationship, Isaac now risked asking the question that had been on his mind for three days.

"Father?"

"Yes, my son?" Abraham had known this moment would come.

"The fire and wood are here, Father, but

where is the lamb for the burnt offering?"

Abraham had rehearsed his answer to the boy's question, as much for his own need to hear it as for Isaac's. "God Himself will provide the lamb for the burnt offering, my son."

God Himself will provide. God keeps His promises, Abraham thought, even when it seems impossible. Isaac's very existence was testimony to that. Years ago God had promised to make Abraham into a nation, through Isaac. How could God keep His promise after today?

Abraham's heart pounded and ached. His mouth opened in a silent groan. They had reached the place of sacrifice.

Deliberately Abraham built an altar and laid out the wood. The man and the boy had not spoken since they had arrived, and could not yet inject any words into the tension. Watching his father, Isaac intuitively knew what would happen next. He didn't struggle as his father bound him. Instead, he searched the old man's face for some wordless answer. Father and son locked gazes: one promise, one destiny, one torment.

The knife still hugged Abraham's hip. He closed his hand tightly on its handle and drew it from the warmth of his clothing. As the knife left its sheath, the heat left Abraham's body. Isaac's eyes were closed, his young body rigid. A crescendo mounted in Abraham's chest, and he knew it would end only when the blood of his precious son covered the altar. Against an invisible weight, he raised his arm. Time ceased. Oh, God, why?

"Abraham! Abraham!" A voice penetrated

his agony. "Do not lay a hand on the boy. Do not do anything to him. Now I know that you fear God, because you have not withheld from me your son, your only son." Pounding, heady relief shook Abraham's body. "Abraham looked up and there in a thicket he saw a ram caught by its horns. He went over and took the ram and sacrificed it as a burnt offering instead of his son. So Abraham called that place 'The Lord will provide'" (Genesis 22:13-14).

+   +   +

Four days earlier, God had spoken and Abraham had heard: "Then God said, 'Take your son, your only son Isaac, whom you love, and go to the region of Moriah. Sacrifice him there as a burnt offering on one of the mountains I will tell you about'" (Genesis 22:2).

Abraham had obeyed God because he revered God. Abraham's response to the command showed the attitude of his heart. Because of his obedience, we are sure of his reverence.[1]

What would you have done that day on Mount Moriah?

A test usually reveals a true condition. God's test of Abraham revealed his spiritual heart condition as surely as a doctor's stress test reveals a patient's physical heart condition. Our actions in a test are a far more accurate reading of our soul's state than our words are. While we say, "Lord, Lord," are we doing what He says (Luke 6:46)? In the test times our hearts are revealed.

So it was with Abraham. His "stress test"

revealed that, in his innermost being, Abraham revered God. He expressed this reverence by doing what God told him to do. I am not suggesting that his obedience was easy. Far from it: The carrying out of God's command tore savagely at his only dream and put deepest human affection on the line. Yet, although his obedience was desperately diffi-cult, Abraham didn't vote on it. He walked onto that mountain without looking back because his heart was rooted in his personal reverence of God. Obedience was the fruit of that reverence.

God intends that the committed and reverent heart be expressed in the obedient life. Specific obedience to the Word of God is the fruit of our love for Him. What's more, that fruit is sweet to God and draws Him closer to us in intimacy. In John 14, verses 21 and 23 spell out our obedience and God's response in intimate terms: "Whoever has my commands and obeys them, he is the one who loves me. He who loves me will be loved by my Father, and I too will love him and show myself to him. . . . and we will come to him and make our home with him."

To draw nearer to God and to show Him our love, we are to keep His Word.

This truth was my first discovery in the search for a biblical understanding of obedience: We love God by obeying God. In asking people, "How can we show our love to God?" I have received many imaginative answers, mostly re-flecting a vague, rather ethereal perspective: "by giving Him my whole heart"; "by being who He wants me to be"; "by living a praiseful life"; "by making Him Number One." These are great ideas, but they are still in the realm of a nebulous heart experience, devoid of specifics to act on.

Obeying God, on the other hand, is thought of as something that "dedicated" Christians and missionaries and pastors do well, while the rest of us just try! Thinking that separates loving God and obeying God is a trap of Satan, designed to discourage and frustrate sincere Christians through misunderstanding. As long as we do not understand that we love God by keeping His Word, we will not be deliberately carrying out the greatest commandment:

> Love the Lord your God with all your heart and with all your soul and with all your mind and with all your strength. (Mark 12:30)

As we shall see in the chapters that follow, loving God is not a nebulous heart experience, but a concrete and active expression of commitment through obedience. God has shown us how to love Him by showing us how to obey Him. This is so exciting: I can learn to express love to God in the way He wants me to, by learning how to be actively obedient to Him.

Loving and obeying God are not reserved for those extraordinary Christians who know the Scriptures inside and out and glow with closeness to God. Loving Him, obeying Him, and becoming intimate with Him are for you and me, the ordinary ones, who struggle with sin and selfishness, who are in various stages of familiarity with the

Bible, who want to try but don't know how. What incredibly good news!

Not only can we love God, but we can also keep on growing in that love consistently. Imagine the pleasure that our growing love will give to the heart of God!

How does love for God grow? John tells us how in 1 John 2:5: "But if anyone obeys his word, God's love is truly made complete in him." Jesus gives us a clear illustration of this principle in the parable of the talents. One truth is that the talent-holder must use what he has to get more. The master in the parable praised the servants who had operated on this principle (see Matthew 25:14-30).

In the business world, this principle of using what you already have to get more is called investment. In business this can be risky, but not with God. If we use the budding love we have for God in obedience, He will increase our love. We continue to obey Him; He continues to increase our love. It's a guaranteed investment! Since everyone who is born of God loves God, we all have something to start with, however feeble. God is waiting to grow and strengthen our love for Him.

Whenever I take the opportunity to actively love God in personal obedience, I end up sensing a new tenderness in my heart toward Him and a stronger resolve to obey again next time. Obedience is not an end, but a means—a means to express our love to God, and a means to increase our love for God. It is a catalyst in the process of loving God and becoming more like Jesus.

A catalyst brings about a change that wouldn't

occur without its presence. I learned a memorable lesson about catalysts in a basement chemistry lab. The first time I had to do a chemistry experiment on my own, I was afraid I'd blow the place up. I followed directions to the letter. Soon I held a test tube full of a deep turquoise liquid. The color was dazzling as I held the tube up to the light. But beautiful turquoise liquid was not what I was supposed to end up with.

The directions included two questions about the end product: What color is the solid? Why is the liquid yellow? Hmmm. I checked my neighbor's directions and realized I had missed copying one line off the board. I needed to add a single drop of another substance, a catalyst, to my mixture. I did. The tube warmed up, tiny silver granules formed at the bottom, and the liquid above turned pale yellow. The change amazed me.

God is interested in transforming your life, and obedience is the catalyst He calls you to introduce to the process of becoming more like Jesus. The change will amaze you!

Abraham's obedience on Mount Moriah was not an isolated expression of devotion to God. It was a pivotal incident among a myriad of similar but less costly opportunities to obey. Our first glimpse of Abraham's willingness to obey God is in Genesis 12, where we read that he left his country and moved on at God's command. Abraham's relationship with Lot demonstrated his growing godliness of character as he repeatedly acted in grace and mercy toward his nephew. And when Sarah's barrenness threatened to turn his hope in God's promise into despair, Abraham chose to believe God in spite of appearances.

Yes Abraham failed—lots of times. But his practice of loving God in obedience had increased and strengthened his reverent heart. When the time of make-or-break testing came, unflinching obedience revealed the love that he and God had cultivated.

When do we practice loving God? In church? When the big decisions loom? When all else fails? I certainly hope we would practice loving God in those situations. However, those are not the times when most of the practice sessions occur. Like Abraham, we must practice loving God during the minutes of the everyday, through the hours of the ordinary. That's when we obey God and grow in our love for Him. Then when those times of tough decisions, fierce temptations, and overwhelming storms come—and they will—the tests will reveal our true commitment. As any athlete can testify, the brief competition under the lights only displays what has been cultivated in the routine and hidden moments of the daily workout.

The understanding and skills we gain concerning obedience will help us to practice loving God by obeying His Word in the ordinary and extraordinary moments of the rest of our lives.

Notes
1. Reverence, defined from a combination of sources, is a sense of fear and respect together with an adoring awe and tenderness of feeling.

2
The Character of Obedience: What Does God Tell Us?

The aerialist focuses on a point at the far end of the tightrope and uses skill and balance to master the crossing.

The orchestra musicians perform before thousands, but see only one: the conductor. Without that focus on the maestro, the musicians would create not music, but chaos.

The photographer creates art when he is fascinated not by his camera, but rather by what he wants to bring into focus.

Focused on God
In the same way, the Christian who wants to live obediently must focus on God at all times. This is the primary characteristic of obedience: eyes on

21

God. The author of Hebrews likens the Christian life to a race. He summons us to "fix our eyes on Jesus" (Hebrews 12:2) as we run. After all, who else is the race for?

In the Old Testament Book of Deuteronomy, multiple chapters record the nature and content of obedience. Blessings, curses, possibilities, and promises abound. A thoughtful reader of the book is struck by the care God took to insure that His people understood what He meant when He said He wanted them to obey. Then, in chapter 30, verses 19 and 20, the writer summarized, bringing the importance of obedience to a head:

> This day I call heaven and earth as witnesses against you that I have set before you life and death, blessings and curses. Now choose life, so that you and your children may live and that you may love the LORD your God, listen to his voice, and hold fast to him. For the LORD is your life, and He will give you many years in the land he swore to give to your fathers, Abraham, Isaac and Jacob.

Think back to Abraham. How could he raise the knife to kill Isaac, his son of promise? Was his obedience blind? No. Abraham focused on who God is—a God of the miraculous—and knew that God would keep His promise to bless the earth through his offspring, even if it meant raising Isaac from the dead. God's character provided Abraham's hope.

God's character provides our hope. We may

not feel that we are in control of our situation, but God is in control. That is hope. We may not have energy and ability enough to carry out our responsibilities, but God is all-powerful and fully able to enable us step by step. That is hope. We may be shocked and reeling from an overwhelming storm, but God is the unmoving Rock beneath us, ready to be our help and refuge in the midst of our storm. That is hope.

The depth of who God is and the breadth of all He has done form the limits for our focus and the basis for our hope. Looking at Him and becoming aware of His character as related to our situation, we will find that our needs fall into perspective.

My camera has a focusing ring that allows me to choose what image will be central in the photograph. It didn't take me long to realize that if I draw one image *into* focus, I automatically put several others *out of* focus. Although there are ways to increase the focusing range, I rather like having a good part of the picture slightly fuzzy; it encourages singular attention. The crisp central focus leaves no doubt about what is important to me in the picture. The result is perspective.

God reveals Himself in the Bible. He says to us, "Seek My face." As we look to Him, we can answer with David, "Your face, LORD, will I seek" (Psalm 27:8). The focus of the loving and obedient heart is the God who first loved us.

I am talking about our chosen response to God. Whenever we zero in on our response to Him, there exists the subtle danger of "formulizing" the Christian life. And any time we think we have hold of a workable formula, we want to revert our trust and attention to the formula, losing our focus on God. In this way, we end up trusting in praise rather than in God; or believing that prayer changes things rather than God.

Obedience is not a formula; rather, it is the attitude of a person who looks at God and says, "I want to follow You. I will do as You say, because I love You and want above all else to please You." With this heart attitude we bring every effort to bear on applying the Scriptures to the walk and talk of our days. That is a focus on God.

Active

The second essential attribute of obedience is that it's active. Consider Philippians 2:12:

> Therefore, my dear friends, as you have always obeyed—not only in my presence, but now much more in my absence—continue to work out your salvation with fear and trembling.

Our obedient walk is God's way of actively involving us in our sanctification.

Many of us both desire and intend to actively obey God. Our problem is how—*how* do we actively obey God? Our vague efforts usually miss the mark, and even our strongest intentions often end in fizzled attempts and short-lived changes. Along the road of following God we lodge at the twin cities of Sincere Intention and Trying Hard. And the place is crowded! We can see the road winding out beyond these stopping points, but we hear little of what lies out there.

Most of us desire to pull up stakes from the twin cities and press on. The pressing on is accomplished one step at a time. The difference between staying *in* Intention and Trying, and setting out *from* those familiar lodgings, is in *steps of action.*

Noah is an amazing example of acting on what God said to him. Although arks were unheard-of, God told Noah to build one. He also told him how and why. Now Noah didn't turn around and go to a seminar on ark-building. Nor did he investigate other people's experience in the construction field. We have no evidence that he spent long stretches in prayer over the right time to start. And he didn't begin preaching to others about the necessity of ark-building. He just *did* it! God's instructions to Noah conclude at the end of verse 21 of Genesis 6. Verse 22 says, "Noah did everything just as God commanded him."

I suspect that if we put half as much energy into doing what God says as we do into innovative efforts to keep out of the realm of action, we'd turn our world upside down! In his excellent book *Loving God,* Chuck Colson expresses his parallel concern:

> My question then, for individual believers and thus for the church, is this: do we view our faith as a magnificent philosophy or a living truth; as an abstract, sometimes academic theory or a living person for whom we are prepared to lay

down our lives? . . . What would happen if we
were actually to apply God's truth for the glory
of His kingdom?[1]

The result would be a world revolutionized by the
power of God working through individual Christians and the Church as a whole.

An active response to His Word pleases God.
In a culture where blood relationships and family
loyalties determined destinies, Jesus shocked His
hearers with this astounding assertion: "My mother
and brothers are those who hear God's word and
put it into practice" (Luke 8:21). Jesus rewards
the doers of His Word with the intimacy of the
closest relationship possible. This is the relationship for which we were created.

By contrast, an inactive response to God's
instruction does not please Him, because it is not
obedience. *It is disobedience*. What painful truth!
There is no middle ground: Once I have heard the
Lord speak, I either act on it or I don't. I either
obey or I disobey.

Like the teenager who left for the evening
without inquiring about curfew so that he might
plead ignorance upon returning late, so many
Christians avoid the Bible, hoping not to have to
deal with the issues that might arise. I have met
scores of Christians who, while insisting on their
desire for God, consistently refuse to become
involved in the personal study of His Word. It is
much easier to live a Christian lifestyle than to act
on a specific challenge from the Word of God.

James writes that if we are hearers of the

Word without being doers of it, we deceive ourselves. Revelation 3:14-18 describes this self-deception. The Laodicean church rated itself right up there at the top, rich and without needs. Yet Jesus said its people were totally unaware of their true wretchedness. They were self-deceived. How did they get into such a state? By being "lukewarm"; they neither actively followed God, nor actively rejected Him. Their response to God was apathetic, and Jesus said, "So, because you are lukewarm—neither hot nor cold—I am about to spit you out of my mouth" (Revelation 3:16).

God doesn't want us to miss this point: Obedience is active.

Personal

The Bible adds another dimension to our understanding of obedience: It is personal. Romans 14:12 tells us that "each of us will give an account of himself to God." Each person's response to God thrills Him because it is unique. He enjoys us as He has made us—different from all others. And He has set the pace for our personal response by dealing individually with us. Your need and mine at this moment may be as varied as night and day, yet God meets each of us completely, in the place and time fitted to us. Our obedience yields the same personal response to Him. This is one-to-one relating with God.

An old man is speaking in 1 Kings 2:1-4. David is on his deathbed, uttering his last words to Solomon, his son and Israel's new king. Father charges son to "observe," "walk in," and "keep" the commands of God. David's God-pleasing life didn't cover Solomon; he had to enact his own obedience. David knew that and spoke earnestly to the new king of his responsibility to obey. Unfortunately, Solomon eventually allowed his own desires to outweigh his commitment to obey God.

In a very real sense, we each stand or fall alone. Those closest to us may encourage, challenge, support, help, and pray for us, but we act on our own choice. Even the Holy Spirit, the Christian's constant Companion, Teacher, Comforter, and Enabler, will not act for us. No one can do our obeying but we ourselves. Husbands cannot obey for their wives, or vice versa. Parents cannot credit their walk with God to their children, nor a pastor credit his intimacy with God to his congregation. God individually calls each soul, speaks to each mind, whispers in each ear, when He says, "Obey my voice."

All-encompassing

Occasionally I meet someone who has divided the Scriptures into two distinct categories: "what applies to me" and "what doesn't apply to me." The division surpasses the obvious (such as Ephesians 5:22-33 not applying directly to the unmarried), and winds on through the pages of the Bible, conveniently relegating the uncomfortable portions to the "doesn't-apply-to-me" category. What this person admits to openly, many of us do unconsciously.

Yet the Bible itself makes it clear that we are to obey God fully (Exodus 19:5). Obedience is all-encompassing. Jesus, in Matthew 28:20, instructs His disciples to teach others "to obey *everything* I have commanded you." We cannot pick and choose. We all have the self-serving tendency to screen the Word of God to one degree or another. Instinctively we ignore the portions that might unsettle our lives too much. In doing so, we plant seeds of needless pain for the future.

When God brought His people into the Promised Land, His instruction to them included an unequivocal command to eradicate the land's existing occupants. Knowing Israel's penchant to obey what they wanted to and ignore the rest, the Lord gave them this warning: "But if you do not drive out the inhabitants of the land, those you allow to remain will become barbs in your eyes and thorns in your sides. They will give you trouble in the land where you will live" (Numbers 33:55).

Saul, King of Israel two centuries later, was cut from the same cloth. Samuel the priest gave Saul strict orders from God to completely destroy the Amalekites. Saul allowed himself and the people some "small and reasonable exceptions," which he had convinced himself were in God's best interests. In Saul's mind, these exceptions didn't reflect any departure from God's command (see 1 Samuel 15). But God did not accept Saul's reasoning. Incomplete obedience is disobedience. When Samuel confronted Saul, his conclusion was agonizingly final: "Because you have rejected the word of the LORD, he has rejected you as king" (1 Samuel 15:23).

God's injunction for us to obey Him fully is

not for His benefit but for ours. He desires to give, not to get. That was not the picture of God that a young coed had when I spoke to her about commitment to Christ. Her reply? "I'm a Christian, but I'm going to wait a while before I dedicate my life to the Lord. I need to have some fun first!"

God is not out to spoil our fun. Read Exodus 19:5 and Deuteronomy 15:4 and 5. Then turn to chapter 28 of Deuteronomy, verses 1-14. The list of blessings is breathtaking! God is determined to demonstrate to us that full obedience will bring gain, not loss. His promise is that "whoever loses his life for my sake will find it" (Matthew 10:39). What looks (and sometimes feels) like a loss becomes a gain. There is no doubt that obedience is costly, but a multiple return on our investment is guaranteed (see Mark 10:28-30).

I have struggled for a long time with a strong allergic reaction to conflict. In my effort to avert or avoid conflict, I have withdrawn, lied, compromised, and repressed feelings. As God began to speak to me about changing my pattern, I was petrified. "Whoever loses his life" was an apt phrase for me because in conflict I felt totally unprotected and vulnerable. To walk into and through a major conflict in some area of my life seemed tantamount to a death sentence. Yet I knew I was sinning in the pattern I held to. Both options were so abhorrent to me that I wanted to evaporate into thin air.

That not being possible, by the grace of God I chose to change my pattern. I chose to step into conflict and confrontational situations as they came up and to speak calmly and remain honest in them. For awhile I felt as though I were drowning. Gradually I have discovered the situations are manageable, although unpleasant. God has turned my terror into a realistic acceptance of conflict, and has even taught me to use the opportunities to learn, grow, and sometimes minister to another. I am still learning. And God and I are closer for the journey through it together.

Not only does God intend for us to obey Him fully, but also to do so with our whole heart—*all* of what God says with *all* our heart:

> Love the Lord your God with all your heart and with all your soul and with all your mind. (Matthew 22:37)

These words are so familiar to us that we forget they speak of the very yearning of God. He created us for Himself and He longs to draw the response of our whole heart to Him. The little booklet *My Heart, Christ's Home*, written by Dr. Robert Munger,[2] beautifully illustrates how God wants full access to every part of our life. Its author describes our heart as a house where Christ longs to be Master. But He lets us hand over the private corners and major rooms to His control.

It is up to us to make Him "at home" in our life, not as guest but as owner. We say we want God in control of our heart. Then let's fling open the door, lay bare the dark corners, stop clutching our "pet sins," and allow everything to come under the scrutiny of Scripture. And when our

Master points to a mess that needs cleaning up or an area that lacks beauty, let's pour ourselves into following His kind direction.

Immediate

Obedience is also immediate. God will speak to you today about what He wants you to do today. Even when He directs concerning future plans or patterns, there will be implications for the present. If God brings something to your attention, He expects you to begin the process of looking after it. Procrastination of obedience is disobedience.

David had learned this truth, probably the hard way! In Psalm 119:67, he recalls, "Before I was afflicted I went astray, but now I obey your word." He had developed a new pattern of responding to God's Word, as he describes in Psalm 119:60: "I will hasten and not delay to obey your commands."

Some years ago our family spent a summer at Glen Eyrie, conference grounds and international headquarters for The Navigators. At lunch one day, we had the privilege of being joined by Lila Trotman, widow of Dawson Trotman, the founder of The Navigators. We were listening intently to her response to a question. Suddenly, in mid-sentence, she stopped, put her hand on mine, and spoke to me in a low and urgent voice. "Is that your little boy?" I followed her eyes and saw three-year-old Nathan playing in some tall grass just beyond the courtyard. I nodded yes. "Then go and get him this instant!" Without stopping to ask why, I jumped up and ran to bring Nathan back to our group. When I returned, Mrs. Trotman smiled at me and looked tenderly at Nathan. "I'm glad you went without delay," she said, "We have killed many rattlers in that very patch. I just wanted your son to be safe."

We delay acting on the truth to our own detriment. Of the unfortunate people who are diagnosed with lung cancer each year, at least 90 percent can trace their disease to smoking.[3] Yet I would be surprised if even one of those people could claim innocence about the hazards of smoking. There are warnings on every cigarette pack, in every cigarette ad, and in the newspaper and magazine reports across the nation. Yet, for these people, the warnings became meaningless. Even the occasional spurts of good intention to stop smoking were quickly stolen by the thief procrastination, and each smoker puffed his or her way into the cancer statistics. Delay spelled disaster.

We need to obey quickly and not risk the hardening of our heart to the admonitions of Scripture. "So, as the Holy Spirit says: 'Today, if you hear his voice, do not harden your hearts as you did in the rebellion, during the time of testing in the desert'" (Hebrews 3:7-8). In Galatians 5:25, Paul reasons that "since we live by the Spirit, let us keep in step with the Spirit." The quick response of obedience keeps us "in step" as God works, by His Spirit, in our life.

Our duty

The Bible leaves no doubt that this obedience we have been describing is also required; in fact, commanded. It is not our option, but our duty. How humbling! We are not doing "extra work," getting "extra credit," when we follow God; we are only doing what is expected of us. "So you also, when you have done everything you were told to do, should say, 'We are unworthy servants; we have only done our duty'" (Luke 17:10).

Our children enjoy playing computer games. Often a game is programmed with different levels of difficulty and/or speed. The player selects from this menu of options based on how much of a challenge he feels like facing. There is no such menu for obedience. While it is true that God carefully tailors His individual challenges to us according to our ability to respond, it does not imply that we have options in our response. If we are to follow God, obedience is our duty.

Possible

These characteristics of obedience are hard words to hear. When we encounter the nature of our responsibility, we also feel the weight of its obligation on our shoulders. That weight might crush us, and its standard would certainly be beyond our reach, if it weren't for the marvelous and total provision of God. In Christ, He has made His nature available to us. In fact, we actually have His nature within us, if we have Christ: "His divine power has given us everything we need for life and godliness through our knowledge of him who called us by his own glory and goodness" (2 Peter 1:3).

Obedience is possible. If we attempt to look down the corridor of the years ahead, even the weeks ahead, the challenge seems too great to bear. But with Jesus, the burden is light, not because it is without cost and pain, but because we do not carry the load alone.

> Now what I am commanding you today is not too difficult for you or beyond your reach. It is not up in heaven, so that you have to ask, "Who will ascend into heaven to get it and proclaim it to us so that we may obey it?" Nor is it beyond the sea, so that you have to ask, "Who will cross the sea to get it and proclaim it to us so we may obey it?" No, the word is very near you; it is in your mouth and in your heart so you may obey it. (Deuteronomy 30:11-14)

Summary

For the purpose of our own understanding, and to clarify the use of the term *obedience* for the remainder of the book, let's compile the characteristics of obedience into a working definition:

> Obedience is the prompt personal response of an available life to God and His Word, always characterized by a focus on God and a commitment to action.

Notes
1. Charles Colson, *Loving God* (Grand Rapids, Michigan: Zondervan Publishing House, 1983), page 16.
2. InterVarsity Press, 1979.
3. "Facts on Lung Cancer," a pamphlet issued by the Canadian Cancer Society.

3
God's Incredible Response to Our Obedience

David paused at the expanse of thick purple drapery that marked the entrance to the tent where the Ark of the Covenant rested. The fabric's rich color and soft texture had become a reminder to him of God's kindness. But today he needed no reminder: he was already overwhelmed by God's unexpected response to last night's idea.

The huge drape breathed out a sweet perfume as David pulled it aside and closed it again behind him. He stopped and stood motionless, enveloped in a sense of his smallness and sinfulness next to God's greatness and holiness. Gratitude swept over him and he wept, briefly and deeply. He sat down and, as he regained his composure, reviewed the last twelve hours in his mind.

Last evening's conversation had gone from routine matters to the deeper concerns of David's heart. He and Nathan had been walking in the courtyard of the palace. The cool night air was especially refreshing after a hot day. David turned thoughtful.

"Nathan, the Lord has done so much for me. And now, on top of everything else, He's given us back the Ark. Look around you, Nathan. Here I am living in this palace, but where do we put the Ark of God? In a tent!"

Nathan recognized David's intention before David could voice it. "Go ahead," Nathan replied. "Go ahead and do what's on your heart, for the Lord is with you."

David wanted to build God a magnificent house, a place of honor. God's honor had always been a passionate concern of David's, and any insult to it was his call to arms. Now his own prosperity, compared to the present treatment of the Ark of God, made him feel that he, a defender of God's honor, was himself dishonoring God. He wanted to right that wrong and provide for the Ark of God's Presence a place that would render appropriate honor.

Hours after the conversation with Nathan, David finally fell asleep, with a myriad of design ideas tumbling over each other in his mind. He even dreamed he was leading a hundred of Israel's best musicians in songs of praise at the completion of construction. When he woke up, some of the songs seemed to have been real; he could still hear them in his mind.

But God had a different plan, and He had told Nathan about it during the night. When Nathan entered the king's presence the next morning, it was to deliver a surprise.

Now, as David sat in the privacy of the tent, he relived the impact that Nathan's word from God had made on him: God had turned the whole idea around. The tent was no dishonor to Him; in fact, God was more determined to build a lineage from David than to have a house built for Himself. As if He hadn't already given David enough, now He was promising David and Israel a future greater than all imagining—a future that would bear influence beyond time and into eternity. The implications were staggering. Nathan had quoted God:

> I have been with you wherever you have gone, and I have cut off all your enemies from before you. Now I will make your name great, like the names of the greatest men of the earth. And I will provide a place for my people Israel and will plant them so that they can have a home of their own and no longer be disturbed. Wicked people will not oppress them anymore, as they did at the beginning and have done ever since the time I appointed leaders over my people Israel. I will also give you rest from all your enemies.
>
> The LORD declares to you that the LORD himself will establish a house for you: When your days are over and you rest with your fathers, I will raise up your offspring to succeed you, who will come from your own body, and I will establish his

> kingdom. . . . Your house and your kingdom
> will endure forever before me; your throne will
> be established forever. (2 Samuel 7:9-12, 16)

Only with difficulty could David grasp the truth that the God who had already given him the kingdom and peace on all sides wanted to bless him further. The reality of God's intention infused David's heart with fresh humility and renewed awe before the Lord his God. Still incredulous, he began to pour out his heart to the Lord:

> Who am I, O Sovereign LORD, and what is my
> family, that you have brought me this far? And as
> if this were not enough in your sight, O Sovereign
> LORD, you have also spoken about the future of
> the house of your servant. Is this your usual way
> of dealing with man, O Sovereign LORD?
>   What more can David say to you? For you
> know your servant, O Sovereign LORD. For the
> sake of your word and according to your will,
> you have done this great thing and made it
> known to your servant. (2 Samuel 7:18-21)

+   +   +

God *had* done many great things for David. He probably didn't know that Samuel had called him "a man after God's own heart" (1 Samuel 13:14), but he was definitely aware that his obedient life elicited a response from God.

When King Saul's pursuit of David finally ended, David knew his deliverance was a blessing from God. And he interpreted it, at least in part, as

God's response to his obedience. In his deliverance song, recorded in Psalm 18, David lists God's love and his own obedience as the two reasons for blessing:

> He brought me out into a spacious place;
> he rescued me because he delighted in me.
> The LORD has dealt with me according to my
>   righteousness;
> according to the cleanness of my hands he has
>   rewarded me.
> For I have kept the ways of the LORD;
> I have not done evil by turning from my God.
> All his laws are before me;
> I have not turned away from his decrees.
> I have been blameless before him
> and have kept myself from sin.
> The LORD has rewarded me according to my
>   righteousness,
> according to the cleanness of my hands in his
>   sight. (Psalm 18:19-24)

Does David's interpretation of God's blessing imply that he felt he had earned a reward from God? Far from it! The wonder he expressed in his tent prayer was characteristic of his reactions to God's blessing. He didn't demand, or expect, circumstantial blessing from God. His obedience, like Abraham's, grew in the garden of his love for God. He was satisfied with God alone as his reward: "You are my LORD; apart from you I have no good Thing" (Psalm 16:2). And when other blessings came, he expressed humble gratitude to God.

How could David link God's blessing to his own obedience without believing that he had actually earned the blessing? We learn the secret of his attitude in Psalm 18:32: "It is God who arms me with strength and makes my way perfect." David knew that even his obedience found its source in God. Only because of God's power could David obey. How could he take the credit when he didn't provide the power?

Oh that we could grasp the mind-set David had! When we obey, it is because God enables us to love Him. When He blesses us, it is because He has chosen to respond to our expression of love to Him. We can never cite our obedience as a reason to demand anything from God. Yet in His love and goodness, God wants to respond to us by blessing our lives "immeasurably more than all we ask or imagine" (Ephesians 3:20).

Our God's nature is responsive. The patterns of God's generous love response to David's obedience are repeated throughout Scripture. He has established spiritual principles that leave us with both hope and warning. Because He is a Responder, He *will respond* to everything we are and do—our obedience and our disobedience alike. In fact, His response goes beyond this life into the next. Second Corinthians 5:9-10 tells us that part of Paul's motivation to please God was his awareness that God ultimately would examine his life and respond accordingly. God's inevitable response and evaluation might help to motivate us in pleasing Him.

David's life provides a panoramic view of

how God responds to the obedient person. In David's history and in the heartbeat of the psalms he wrote, God's patterns of response to obedience are revealed.

Intimacy

David's obedience took him into the caves of Jerusalem's surrounding mountains. Because he refused to lift a hand against Saul—"the LORD's anointed," as David referred to him—he was forced to flee the murderous king. Months of running stretched into years. Distressed and alone, David cried out to God in encounter after encounter, "What should I do?" In one such instance, even his own men questioned him (see 1 Samuel 23). But God always answered clearly, and David always obeyed faithfully.

As those years filled with battles, loneliness, danger, and uncertainty were spending themselves, God was responding to David's sacrifice of obedience. The process had begun in the fields when young David had lived out days, even weeks, isolated with his sheep, far from home. God began then to give the fruit of intimacy in response to David's faithful trust. God and David grew deeper in their closeness through the years that followed until God could say, "Here is a man after my own heart," and David could say, "And I—in righteousness I will see your face; when I awake, I will be satisfied with seeing your likeness" (1 Samuel 13:14 and Psalm 17:15).

To know God. To hunger and thirst for more of Him. To be able to say with Paul, "I consider everything a loss compared to the surpassing greatness of knowing Christ Jesus my Lord" (Philippians 3:8). Is this not the deep longing of our hearts as we follow God? As we obey Him, our Lord's response to us will parallel His response to David: "Whoever has my commands and obeys them, he is the one who loves me. He who loves me will be loved by my Father, and I too will love him and show myself to him" (John 14:21).

Solomon must have observed the outstanding blessing of intimacy with God in David's life, because in Proverbs 3:32 (NASB) he says, "For the crooked man is an abomination to the LORD; but He is *intimate with the upright.*" What a promise!

Impact

The Apostle Paul summarized the life of David well when he told the people at Antioch that "David . . . served God's purpose in his own generation" (Acts 13:36). Israel imitated her king. Because of one man's obedient life, a whole nation learned to please God. In fact, the people from then on referred to God as "The God of David." Every king of Israel who came after David was measured against him.

Not only was David God's means to influence a nation, and God's measure for all of the nation's future kings, but he was also the first in the lineage that would culminate in the coming of Christ the Messiah.

Centuries later, David's impact had stood the test of time. He was still called a man after God's own heart (Acts 13:22). Jerusalem was still the

City of David. God was still the God of David.
And Christ had come as the Seed of David.

Add nineteen more centuries, during which
thousands upon thousands have read David's
psalms and found his life and writing to be a
ministry in their lives. Sufferers have gone peace-
fully to their deaths, comforted by Psalm 23.
Wanderers have repented through Psalm 51.
Strugglers have affirmed their confidence in God
as they have identified with words like these:

> As for God, his way is perfect;
>> the word of the LORD is flawless.
> He is a shield
>> for all who take refuge in him.
> For who is God besides the LORD?
>> And who is the Rock except our God?
> It is God who arms me with strength
>> and makes my way perfect. (Psalm 18:30-32)

Questioners have sought guidance with David:
"Show me the way I should go, for to you I lift up
my soul" (Psalm 143:8). And worshipers have
sung praises recorded in dozens of David's psalms.
Twenty-nine centuries of influence, and still his
impact continues!

Imagine the satisfaction David would have
experienced, knowing he was turning others Godward. "Come, my children," he says in Psalm 34.
"Listen to me; I will teach you the fear of the
LORD." To see God bring forth the fruit of influence from his own obedient heart and work would
have been a thrilling answer to the longing of his

heart: "O Israel, put your hope in the LORD both now and forevermore" (Psalm 131:3).

God has chosen to bless the obedient individual by using his or her life to influence others for eternity. You and I are not kings, but God responds to us just as He did to David. As we obey Him, who we are and what we do will have a breadth of impact that only eternity will reveal.

God allows our obedience to trigger His touch in all our relational circles. He blesses our children (Psalm 112:1-2), ministers to our spouses (1 Peter 3:1), builds up the Body of Christ (Ephesians 4:15-16), brings honor to Himself (Matthew 5:16), gives many an appetite to know God (2 Corinthians 2:14-15), and draws unbelievers to Christ (Acts 9:32-35).

We carry within us the Person of the Lord Jesus. As we walk obediently with Him, serving Him in His plan, He reaches out through us to others, often in ways that are unknown to us or outlive us.

As a youngster, I had a pen pal in the Malaysian Air Force. Teo Seng Wah was a Christian youth who was not hesitant to align himself openly with Christ. Disowned by his family because of his Christian commitment, he still gently persisted in meeting their needs whenever he could. Several months after our correspondence slowed to a stop, I received a letter from Seng Wah's friend in the Air Force. Seng Wah had been killed in a plane crash during routine duty. The letter outlined the broad influence of his humble life. And then I read these words: "His mother and father and all his brothers and sisters, except one, have come to Christ because of his life."

We cannot measure God's response to our obedience based only on the results *we* see. The last years of David's life were marred by family discord, exile, illness, the rebellion and death of his son Absalom, and rivalry over the inheritance of the kingdom. Some of this trouble was the result of David's sin. At some points, he could probably not see past the distresses to the benefits God was producing from his life. He was undoubtedly far more aware of the fruit of his sin than the fruit of his righteousness.

But David's experience with God kept him from living according to what he could *see*, and thus yielding to discouragement and perhaps disobedience. Instead, he fixed his focus again on God, even though it was often blurred by tears, and drew confidence that God was doing a lot more than what he could see. Listen to the psalm David wrote as he fled from his violent and rebellious son Absalom:

> But you are a shield around me, O LORD,
>   my Glorious One, who lifts up my head.
> To the LORD I cry aloud,
>   and he answers me from his holy hill. . . .
> From the LORD comes deliverance.
>   May your blessing be on your people.
>   (Psalm 3:3-4, 8)

Sometimes, when we look around us, all we see is a mess. Perhaps, like Asaph in Psalm 73, we have tried to serve and please God only to find an apparent vacuum where we'd hoped to see results. From our vantage point, we are hard pressed to come up with one positive influence that has come from our obedience. But God is at work far beyond our limited scope of vision, and we must cling to that truth in faith. We must not "become weary in doing good, for at the proper time we will reap a harvest if we do not give up" (Galatians 6:9).

Bob Boardman is a contemporary example of a man who would not give up, but continued in faithful obedience to his Lord's leading. A Navigator missionary to Japan, Bob held on to a promise from God that He would bring fruit from Bob's efforts to spread the gospel in that country. Year after agonizing year passed with no visible results. Some encouraged Bob to try a different mission field, but he knew God wanted him in Japan. Persevering in the face of discouragement and lack of support, Bob believed and obeyed God. *Several years later* God broke open the fruit basket, fulfilling His promise, and beginning a spiritual lineage that long ago grew beyond counting.

God responds to our enduring obedience, allowing us to have a supernatural impact on the world around us, even when we are not aware of it.

Transformation

God's third pattern of response to our obedience is our transformation. Second Corinthians 3:18 says that "we, who with unveiled faces all reflect the Lord's glory, are being transformed into his likeness with ever-increasing glory, which comes from the Lord, who is the Spirit."

David could have become an arrogant, aggressive king, embittered by Saul's past treatment and bent on revenge. He could have used his wealth selfishly and oppressed the people in his power. We have the record of many kings of Israel who did just that. Why didn't David become such a king? He answers the question in Psalm 16:8: "I have set the LORD always before me. Because he is at my right hand, I will not be shaken."

David kept his focus on God, and God's response was to permanently transform David's life. David did not set out to become a man of God; he set out to know and please God. But he *did* become a man of God, because God transformed him into one. Did David's obedience transform his life? Absolutely not! God alone transforms lives.

If we seek the transformed life, we will go to our graves in frustration. But if we seek to know and obey God, we will discover that He is changing us to be more like Jesus, because God has chosen to do so in response to our commitment to Him.

Transformation is not an event; it is a process—a process that God will continue until He completes it in Heaven. When David observed the characteristics of his life as it was being transformed, he overflowed with enthusiastic praise and happy gratitude to God.

The characteristics of a life-in-transformation are blessings within a blessing. David describes them for us:

LORD, you have assigned me my portion and
                my cup;
    you have made my lot secure.
The boundary lines have fallen for me in
                pleasant places;
    surely I have a delightful inheritance.
I will praise the LORD, who counsels me;
    even at night my heart instructs me.
I have set the LORD always before me.
    Because he is at my right hand,
    I will not be shaken.
Therefore my heart is glad and my tongue
                rejoices;
    my body also will rest secure,
because you will not abandon me to the grave,
    nor will you let your Holy One see decay.
You have made known to me the path of life; you
    will fill me with joy in your presence, with
    eternal pleasures at your right hand.
                                (Psalm 16:5-11)

David says that God gave him a bedrock
personal security (verses 5 and 8). In other psalms
David praises God for having taken him from a
slippery place and set him on a rock (for example,
Psalm 40:2). What is this security of which David
writes? He tells us in Psalm 138:8: "The LORD
will fulfill his purpose for me; your love, O LORD,
endures forever."

David's certainty was based not on circumstances, but on the character of God and the
nature of His response to His obedient children.
As God transforms our lives, we too will find

ourselves growing in that unshakable security that is founded in who God is. God Himself will increasingly become our anchor. Our relationships, our jobs, our health, our finances—these are all easily threatened in the waves of time and circumstances. But the grace and power of God, and His desire and ability to bring His intentions to pass in all that occurs, are eternally unchanging. This is security.

Another characteristic of the life-in-transformation is the presence of godly wisdom. David testifies to God's continuous counsel. In Psalm 119:100, he claims to have understanding beyond his years as a result of obeying the Word of God.

We all want wisdom to make today's big decisions. But the wisdom God promises goes far deeper than the urgent issues that capture our attention. It reaches and directs our attitudes, thoughts, and perspectives in the midst of life's smorgasbord of people and experiences. This is not a wisdom gained from the normal lessons of life. It is a blessing God gives to the obedient: "For the LORD gives wisdom, and from his mouth come knowledge and understanding. He holds victory in store for the upright, he is a shield to those whose walk is blameless" (Proverbs 2:6-7).

What else did David observe about the changes God was making in his life? Look again at the passage from Psalm 16 (page 50). David asserts that when he is in God's presence, God fills him with joy. When is he in God's presence? *All the time!* David set the LORD *always* before him (verse 8). God filled David with joy constantly—

even during periods of desperation. Psalm 4 was written in the context of great distress. Yet verse 7 reveals David's amazing state of heart underneath the emotion of the trial: "You have filled my heart with greater joy than when . . . grain and new wine abound."

What is this kind of joy that David could claim when his companions were threats, danger, and disillusionment? The Hebrew word for joy used in Psalm 4:7 is almost identical in meaning to the root of the Greek word James uses when he encourages us to "consider it pure joy, my brothers, whenever you face trials of many kinds, because you know that the testing of your faith develops perseverance" (James 1:2). This word means "cheerfulness" and "mirth." God actually transforms the hearts of His obedient children, surprising us as we begin to find our cheerfulness bubbling up through dark situations.

Mirth implies a sense of humor. I think God increasingly matures our sense of humor and blesses us with an ability to chuckle at the earthiness of our plight from the perspective of eternity. David describes this transformation in Psalm 30:11-12: "You turned my wailing into dancing; you removed my sackcloth and clothed me with joy, that my heart may sing to you and not be silent. O LORD my God, I will give you thanks forever."

Perhaps you have known someone, as I have, whose joy in a desperate or painful circumstance amazed and ministered to others. What a credit to the transforming work of God that He willingly, lovingly develops such a supernatural response in His obedient child! This joy will increasingly be part of our lives as we obey Him. Centuries ago, David had all God's faithful ones in mind when he wrote:

> But let all who take refuge in you be glad;
>   let them ever sing for joy.
> Spread your protection over them,
>   that those who love your name may rejoice
>   in you.
> For surely, O LORD, you bless the righteous;
>   you surround them with your favor as with
>   a shield. (Psalm 5:11-12)

God has chosen to respond to our obedience by giving to us. And what are His gifts? They are the very desires of our hearts: to know Him intimately, to serve Him effectively, and to become like Him increasingly. I believe David had these blessings in mind when he assured us in Psalm 37:4, "Delight yourself in the LORD and he will give you the desires of your heart."

4
What Hinders Our Steps?
Factors that Keep Us from Obeying

The morning mist had lifted. I remember shading my eyes with my hand and focusing on the jut of land, 1½ miles down the beach, that would be my turnaround point on a 3-mile run. Suddenly my feet ached, my legs felt heavy, and I longed to sit down. Just *anticipating* the steps ahead tired me out! Thanks to the encouragement of my enthusiastic family, I did not sit down, but started running, and for the first time in my life completed a 3-mile course.

When the fog dissipates and the meaning of the long stretch of obedience ahead becomes clear, the implications may seem overwhelming. We certainly feel inadequate to the task, and indeed we are in ourselves. Such a response is natural, and shows that we are being realistic about the life to which God has called us. Jesus encouraged a sober effort at cost-counting, because being His disciples will cost us our lives.

Look for a moment at the disciplines of time management and problem solving. Both involve (among other things) breaking down a challenging task, a lengthy time period, or a large problem into its component parts and dealing with those parts one at a time. What seems impossible becomes possible. The overwhelming becomes manageable. The challenge becomes deeply satisfying.

Steps are the smallest pieces of a long journey. Obedience is a long journey: Loving God is a lifelong pursuit. The Christian life is often referred to as a walk. And notice how the psalmist's determination to follow God is expressed in terms of careful steps: "Direct my footsteps according to your Word; let no sin rule over me" (Psalm 119:133).

God wants to teach us lifelong obedience by directing our steps—not just for the miles, but for the inches as well. It is in this daily, volitional alignment of my walk with God's Word that I practice obedience—*one step at a time*. These steps of application are the small pieces that, put one after another, make up my journey as I follow God.

Unfortunately, few of us have been taught to focus on the steps. Instead, we shade our spiritual eyes and wilt as we stare down the long road of enduring commitment. Resolve and reluctance become tangled together, and we lose the gladness of our pursuit. We desperately hope we won't drop out when the going gets tough. But since we hardly know how to live out today's commitment, it's worrisome to envision what might test our walk tomorrow.

But because God knew this realistic perspective would also be potentially paralyzing, He set about to teach us to undertake obedience *one step at a time*. His challenge to us is to view the road ahead from a what's-the-next-step perspective. If the road ahead is intimidating, God's method is not: Take it one step at a time.

But a crucial question remains: If God is willing to direct our steps, why do we still remain inert? Why are we not moving forward in active commitment? Indeed, a heart-rending characteristic of the evangelical world today is that daily obedience to God is the exception, not the rule.

Why is this so?

Substitution

One reason for our inertia is that *we allow external conformity to our particular Christian culture to replace obedience to the Word of God*. In Isaiah 29:13, the Lord says, "These people come near to me with their mouth and honor me with their lips, but their hearts are far from me. Their worship of me is made up only of rules taught by men." Outward conformity is obedience with the heart gone from it. In a sense, it is dead obedience. Unfortunately, however, it's often so similar to living obedience that the fraud is mistaken for the real thing by those around us. And tragically, we can even deceive ourselves, thinking that our conformity is the obedience God desires.

While we wouldn't miss a church service, we continue to dislike our neighbor or we carry on a cold war with a loved one. Although we follow the Scripture passages closely during Sunday school and church, our Bibles stay firmly closed the rest of the week. We serve sacrificially on boards and committees, yet are insensitive to the needs of our families. We involve ourselves wholeheartedly in the missions conference, but never talk to someone about Christ. Our tithes land in the offering plate regularly, but our hearts remain greedy. We do not practice inwardly what we do outwardly.

The prophet Samuel was sent by God to Jesse's family to anoint a new king over Israel. When he saw Jesse's son Eliab, Samuel thought for sure that he had found the right man. Imagine his surprise when God corrected him:

> Do not consider his appearance or his height, for I have rejected him. The LORD does not look at the things man looks at. Man looks at the outward appearance, but the Lord looks at the heart. (1 Samuel 16:7)

External conformity is based on standards and rules. The more emphasis we put on our lists of dos and don'ts, even the legitimate ones, the greater is the danger of breeding merely cultural Christian conformity. A heavy emphasis on dutiful behavior can lead to a neglect of the heart. In many Christian settings we are encouraged to conform. But in how many settings are we actually *taught*—not just *told*—to obey?

Do I imply that all conformity is amiss? Of course not! Conformity based on what God is teaching us daily concerning a life pleasing to Him honors God. But outward conformity that clothes a stagnant walk with God is a dangerous facade.

Why do we slip into allowing shallow conformity to substitute for heart-felt obedience?

One reason is that real spiritual growth is hard work. Conformity allows us to mold our outer life long before our inner life has a chance to catch up. Then we may find our patterns so comfortable that we tend to neglect the heart of the matter altogether. Bible reading, for instance, is a relatively easy habit to establish (and a good one, at that!). The *real* work (and benefit) is in putting what we read into action. Unfortunately, many are quite content to stop at reading, satisfied that they have settled into a good Christian habit.

Another reason that we are tempted to substitute outer conformity for inner obedience is that behavioral conformity gains for us instant acceptance, approval, even status, with others. The teenager who toes the line faithfully is held up as a model to the others, while his or her inner life may be in turmoil without anyone knowing. Outward patterns are false guarantees of any significant inner changes.

A third reason that we permit conformity to replace obedience is that life seems predictable and secure when we can focus on prescribed patterns, even good ones. By comparison, responding to God on a personalized, day-by-day basis appears less manageable. It can be easier just to busy ourselves with spiritual responsibilities. We can faithfully attend church, seminars, and conferences to hear good preaching and teaching from our own pastor as well as other leaders. We can keep the steady Christian life going without actually *doing* what God is telling us to do.

In *The Practice of Godliness*, Jerry Bridges capsulizes this issue of conformity:

> It is possible to be very orthodox in one's doctrine and very upright in one's behavior and still not be godly. Many people are orthodox and upright, but they are not devoted to God; they are devoted to their orthodoxy and their standards of moral conduct.[1]

In an age that beams the biggest spotlight on success, we can trick ourselves into believing that lifestyle conformity is God-pleasing obedience because we substitute a goal of becoming a good Christian for the goal of walking with God. We scramble to imitate the success of our Christian heroes and heroines. Bridges clearly identifies the crux of this issue:

> God must be the very focal point of our lives if we wish to have godly character and conduct. This point cannot be overemphasized. Too many of us focus on the outward structure of character and conduct without taking time to build the

inward foundation of devotion to God. . . . This often results in a cold morality or legalism, or even worse, self-righteousness and spiritual pride. Of course, the foundation of devotion to God and the structure of a life pleasing to God must be developed simultaneously. We cannot separate these two aspects of godliness.[2]

When we consider how behavioral conformity alone affects a person outwardly and leaves his heart unchecked, it's not surprising that many "model" Christians have led lives of conscious or unconscious duplicity, often ending in crime. The uncultivated heart, protected with a cover of conformity to a Christian culture, and left to itself without receiving hard-hitting teaching about obedience, will degenerate from health to sickness. It's just a matter of time.

Confusion

A second reason for our inertia is *confusion over what God is responsible for and what we are responsible for in the business of daily living.*

A bumper sticker proclaims, "Let go and let God." That's a right attitude—*at the right time.* It reflects the fact that we fret and stew long after God has made Himself clear. We may frantically overschedule ourselves in the mistaken belief that we are indispensable. Or we may manipulate a person or situation in order to make it come out "right," when God wants to do something altogether different. For times such as these, the right advice is indeed to "let go and let God."

Our problem of inertia develops from applying this attitude at the wrong time. We try (often unconsciously) to give God the responsibility for what we should be doing ourselves. We "let go and let God" when instead we need to take some action. You'll recognize the language that comes with this condition: "I'm praying about my temper, but it's not getting any better yet." "I asked the Lord to wake me up early for my quiet time, but He didn't. I guess He thinks my sleep is more important right now!" "God just hasn't delivered me from that temptation yet." "Have I made a decision yet? Well, I'm waiting for God to start closing the doors. Whichever one He leaves open—I guess that's the one I'll go through!"

We can be confident that God will do *His* part. But He won't do ours!

The farmer is acutely aware of this kind of division of labor. He prepares the soil, sows the seed, provides other needed attention, and then he waits. And waits. And during the waiting, he feels his powerlessness. He cannot bring rain or sunshine, hold off hail or tornadoes, or prevent premature frost. The ripened crop is a testimony to both the farmer's hard work and the Lord's provision. In the absence of either, there would be no harvest.

We work together with God. Inertia often stops us because we are expecting God to do *our* part, to take our steps for us. We are not bystanders in our own spiritual growth. While only God can transform us, He has called us to be involved in the process. We are told that we must "keep in step with the Spirit" (Galatians 5:25). We *do* have God-ordained responsibilities in becoming like Christ. Let's shoulder our basic responsibilities. God will teach us what else we should take on as we go along.

What are these responsibilities?

1. *We are responsible to take in spiritual food.* "Let the word of Christ dwell in you richly" (Colossians 3:16). How full of the Word we are depends on how much of the Word we eat!

2. *We are responsible to maintain ongoing fellowship with our Lord*: to talk with God, heart to heart; to thank and praise Him; to ask Him about a myriad of things; to struggle in His presence. We are responsible for our share of the communication that goes into a meaningful relationship.

3. *We are responsible to use the resources that God has supplied.* The following short story humorously illustrates the manner in which we sometimes handle the resources God provides.

A man named Smith was sitting on his roof during a flood, and the water was up to his feet. Before long a fellow in a canoe paddled past and shouted, "Can I give you a lift to higher ground?"

"No, thanks," said Smith. "I have faith in the Lord and He will save me."

Soon the water rose to Smith's waist. At this point a motorboat pulled up and someone called out, "Can I give you a lift to higher ground?"

"No, thanks. I have faith in the Lord and He will save me."

Later a helicopter flew by, and Smith was

now standing on the roof with water up to his neck. "Grab the rope," yelled the pilot. "I'll pull you up."

"No, thanks," said Smith. "I have faith in the Lord and He will save me." But after hours of treading water, poor exhausted Smith drowned and went to his reward. As he arrived at the Pearly Gates, Smith met his Maker and complained about this turn of events. "Tell me, Lord," he said, "I had such faith in you to save me and you let me drown. What happened?"

To which the Lord replied, "What do you want from me? I sent you two boats and a helicopter!"[3]

God has already provided all the resources we need to carry out our responsibilities before Him. Second Peter 1:3 assures us, "His divine power has given us everything we need for life and godliness through our knowledge of him who called us by his own glory and goodness." Then verse 5 concludes,

> For this very reason, *make every effort* to add to your faith goodness; and to goodness, knowledge; and to knowledge, self-control; and to self-control, perseverance; and to perseverance, godliness; and to godliness, brotherly kindness; and to brotherly kindness, love.

Because He has made provision, God can and does expect us to live responsibly, doing our part. Using God's resources is *hard work*; that's why

Peter says, "Make every effort." One of the resources God has given us is the ability to think, but who would call disciplined and godly thinking easy? Another resource is the constant availability of our Teacher, the Holy Spirit. Yet being a learner amid the pace of our lives demands effort.

4. *We are responsible to act on what we know.* North American Christians today are information-rich and application-poor. From Sunday schools to seminaries we discuss spiritual information. But examining this information is of little consequence unless our lives are deeply and permanently changed by living it out. James 4:17 warns us, "Anyone, then, who knows the good he ought to do and doesn't do it, sins." And if we know what we should be doing, but we don't know how to go about it, we are responsible to find out.

Actively loving God by lining up with His Word indeed requires "every effort." This is the journey of obedience. Our effort is the responsible assumption of our part of God's travel plan. God will do the rest.

Cost

Some of us hesitate to commit ourselves to obeying Christ because we are afraid of what such a commitment might cost us.

What will it cost?

It will cost us our sin. While it is difficult to change sinful behavior, it is far more difficult to face and change the way sin has affected our attitudes, thinking, perceptions, and beliefs. The process (and it *is* a process) is painful. It involves honest reflection, courage to call sin *sin*, and per-severance to understand and deal with sin patterns at every level—heart, mind, and behavior.

We instinctively withdraw from a purge like this by refusing to see our sin. Actually, we often *do* see it, but we try to give it another name. We call our temper a personality problem, our lust a weakness, our whining a matter of immaturity, and so on.

Psychology has provided many helpful terms, clinically defined, to delve into understanding ourselves. Used in this way, they encourage personal responsibility as part of an understanding and growing process. But used flippantly, to cover for sin we'd rather not see, they have the opposite effect. We may even elevate our sin to a place of spiritual necessity, labeling it our "cross to bear" or our "thorn in the flesh."

All this may be an attempt to shrug off the personal responsibility of change. But if we are honest, sooner or later we see through our games to the seriousness of sin's influence in our life. The needs we see in our behavior are only the tip of the iceberg of sin.

The first element in the cost of obedience is the willingness and work of understanding and dealing with sin and its effects deep in our lives.[4] Many of us simply prefer not to face this process. But God is looking for the repentant heart.

> Draw near to God and he will draw near to you. Cleanse your hands, you sinners, and purify your hearts, you men of double mind. (James 4:8, RSV)

The other major element in the cost of obedience is setting aside our own will in deference to God's will, when the two differ. Unfortunately, we have tended to narrow the concept of God's will primarily to issues of personal choice (what job to take, who to marry, where to live). God's will *is* sometimes minutely specific, but it is also broad and basic.

When we study the Scriptures, we are *learning* God's will. When we carry out the principles of His Word, we are *doing* His will. When we rework our thoughts and attitudes because we believe what He says, we are *living* His will. As we walk in the broad way of the Scriptures, God will often focus our attention on specific opportunities to choose His way as it differs from ours.

These choices are sometimes painful. Nevertheless, God's promise is, "Whoever loses his life for my sake will find it" (Matthew 10:39). And in the process, God works within us so that our will and His become increasingly similar, and we find pleasure in the same things that give God pleasure: "For it is God who works in you to will and to act according to his good purpose" (Philippians 2:13).

However, the cost itself is not the real issue behind our hesitation. Cost rarely deters anyone from obtaining what he perceives is good for him. Then why do we find ourselves stalling as we face the cost of obeying Christ? Under the hesitancy there lies a far more serious problem: Essentially, we do not believe in the goodness of God, and therefore, we do not believe in His good intentions toward us. Larry Crabb, a Christian psychologist and teacher, describes this dilemma:

> Our failure to readily follow His leading reflects a lack of deep confidence in His goodness. We wonder if He is merely using us or wants to bless us. The problem of unsteady commitment is not centrally a problem of the will; it is rather deficient belief. . . . If we *knew* He was good, we would sense a deep desire to follow His leading. . . . Obedience to God's orders deepens our awareness of His goodness, and our awareness of His goodness provides motivation for further obedience. Obedience without an awareness of God's goodness produces a labored commitment that robs us of joy. An awareness of God's goodness that is not coupled with obedience is shallow and will become lifelessly academic. . . . The path He is marking out for us leads to an unparalleled joy for us and glory for Him. An awareness of His character naturally stimulates a desire to follow His leading.[5]

If we shy away from active obedience to God because of what He might require of us, we need to take a fresh look at our loving Lord, step out in application of His Word, and experience His work of deepening our assurance of His thoroughly good and desirable plan for our lives.

Apathy
Is the following description true of you? *The phrase "vital relationship with Christ" has long*

since lost its impact. The awe of God has given way to the rut of duty. Boredom has replaced vibrancy. The Christian life has become ho-hum; "real" life is more exciting.

Underneath it all, if we are painfully honest, is it not this shallow experience of God that robs us of our desire to obey Christ? We may border dangerously on not caring. In a tragic sense, God is no longer real for us. A.W. Tozer, an author and pastor, writes, "For millions of Christians . . . God is no more real than He is to the non-Christian. They go through life trying to love an ideal and be loyal to a mere principle."[6]

Many of us have toughened our spiritual skin, and familiarity has bred in us something akin to contempt. We know so much, yet are so ignorant. Our information bank about spiritual matters is well stocked, but information doesn't give us a rich relationship with God. We go merrily along as our relationship with Jesus Christ is running on a near-zero balance.

Perhaps some of us are in desperate need of a reawakening. The fires of our hearts are reduced to barely glowing coals, and a chill has begun to seep into our bones.

God is a Rekindler. Are you willing to give up your luke-warmness and have your heart-fire stoked? God will fan the coals back into a hearty flame if you put yourself at His disposal and begin to act on His Word. Be honest with Him. Admit your apathy; ask Him to revive your soul. Start feeding on and obeying His Word. He promises to renew your life:

> For this is what the high and lofty One says—
>> he who lives forever, whose name is holy:
> "I live in a high and holy place,
>> but also with him who is contrite and lowly in
>> spirit,
> to revive the spirit of the lowly
>> and to revive the heart of the contrite."
>> (Isaiah 57:15)

God wants us to follow Him. He will direct our footsteps. As we make application of His Word in our lives today, we walk the path of obedience. If we are *not* walking, but merely marking time, it could be that we have focused on outward conformity, we're stalled in confusion, or we've wavered in accepting the cost. Or perhaps we are in need of shedding our dim and dusty view of God and taking on the challenge of a genuine and enlivened relationship with Him.

Will we stand still or move forward? In Exodus 14, the Israelites faced the same question. They had escaped the tyranny of Egypt, but were now trapped between the advancing Egyptian army and the waters of the Red Sea. Death seemed imminent. The people railed at Moses with rage and terror. In the midst of their faithless clamor, God gave Moses a straightforward, three-part directive:

1. The people were to stop panicking.
2. Moses was to stretch his staff over the sea.
3. The people were to move forward.

How did this fickle and frightened mass of refugees respond? Under Moses' leadership, they obeyed the commands of God: *they moved for-*

ward. Did they part the Red Sea? No. They did their part, and *God* did the impossible.

We stand still to our own peril. Let's move forward, step by step, and see God do the impossible. He will open the way before us, enable us to follow Him through the seas, and make us more like Jesus through it all.

> Take my life, and let it be
> Consecrated, Lord, to thee;
> Take my hands, and let them move
> At the impulse of Thy love.
>
> Take my love, my God, I pour
> At Thy feet its treasure store;
> Take myself and I will be
> Ever, only, all for Thee.
>
> Frances Havergal

Notes
1. Jerry Bridges, *The Practice of Godliness* (Colorado Springs: NavPress, 1983), page 45.
2. Bridges, page 67.
3. "Laughter, the Best Medicine," *Reader's Digest*, vol. 124, no. 742, February 1984, pages 49-50.
4. Larry Crabb's *Effective Biblical Counseling* is a very helpful treatment of this vast area.
5. Lawrence J. Crabb, *The Marriage Builder* (Grand Rapids, Michigan: Zondervan Publishing House, 1982), page 116.
6. A.W. Tozer, *The Pursuit of God* (Harrisburg, Pennsylvania: Christian Publications, Inc., 1948), page 50.

5
Hearing God: Knowing and Listening to His Voice

My childhood home was around the corner from a tree-lined field. That meadow has since sprung up in duplexes, but years ago it was the perfect place to let a dog run free for its daily exercise. Many evenings I took my dog Skippy there for an after-supper romp. We both enjoyed the outing, but equally dreaded the roundup that brought it to an end: Skippy knew it meant the loss of her freedom, and I knew I had to chase her in order to catch her. Skippy never seemed to hear me when I called.

Other dog owners had discovered the same field, and most evenings we could be found clustered around the meadow, passing comment on casual matters while our dogs frolicked and barked in exuberant freedom. Most of us had ordinary mutts like Skippy, and had not bothered to train them in any way. When it was time to go, we all chased our pets around the field in an often frustrating effort to hook leash to collar.

There was one man among our group, however, whose relationship with his dog stood out in sharp contrast to the rest of us. When the man was ready to go, he stayed where he was and said, "Come." He didn't speak loudly or use the dog's name, but simply said the word within earshot of his dog. We would all watch in envy and astonishment as one large brown head suddenly lifted from the noisy pack and turned to find the voice. Then this dog would run to his master's side, where he'd sit, panting with the excitement of responding to his master's command, and wait for the leash to be attached. After this impressive performance the rest of us, one by one, would yell and chase until every reluctant dog was on its way home.

Years later, this experience helped me to glimpse some insights into how a person learns to hear the voice of God. One dog in that pack had learned to hear and respond to his master's voice. His training had taken place in private, without the distractions of the noisy field. The result was that even amid the confusion of play, that dog's ear was tuned to his master's word. The dog ignored all other voices and conversations, but he immediately singled out and obeyed his owner's "Come."

Jesus used a similar picture of response when He said, "My sheep listen to my voice; I know them, and they follow Me" (John 10:27). What is involved in hearing the voice of our Master?

The Bible: God's Word to us

The Bible is the only living book in the history of the world. It lives not because it is relevant and full of powerful truth (although it is both of those), but because it is the active voice of our living God, communicating Himself to us. His Person, His character, His ways of dealing with people, His purposes—all remain eternally unchanged and unchanging, revealed in His Word. Not only has God spoken, *He speaks*. He speaks to you and to me today about Himself, about His truth, and about us, His creation. And what He says is indispensable to our lives: "The words I have spoken to you are spirit and they are life" (John 6:63).

Our interaction with God in His word is our private training to recognize and listen to His voice. As we read, hear, study, memorize, and think upon God's Word, our Shepherd's voice becomes more distinct to us, more easily discerned in the din of life. Why, then, do so many of us approach the Scriptures with confusion and leave with frustration or disappointment? Why do we find ourselves unable to hear God speaking to us? Too often the pages seem to hold only printed words. We can't seem to grasp, "*God* is speaking to *me*."

I recall an incident that made me painfully aware of this dilemma in my life. I was riding home from a weekend conference with several acquaintances. One person opened up a review of the weekend by asking each one of us what God had said to us—as individuals. Meaning *me*! In an effort to avoid answering, I suggested we stop for coffee. I had learned a lot of interesting spiritual information at that conference, but God had not, that I could tell, spoken to me personally. I didn't want to admit that underlying my enthusiasm over a wonderful weekend was the sad fact that I had not heard the voice of God.

When Martha and Mary opened their home to Jesus and His disciples (Luke 10:38-42), they demonstrated very different approaches to the speaking Christ. While Martha did the inviting and was obviously glad to have Jesus speaking in her home, *she did not listen to Him.* She made all sorts of preparations, probably related to meal-time, but she was not prepared to hear Jesus. Mary, on the other hand, made the effort to listen to what Jesus was saying: She stopped whatever she was doing and sat at Jesus' feet. Jesus was speaking to both women. Mary heard the voice of God; Martha knew only the frustration of her own predicament. Like Mary, our *availability* and our *attitude* toward God's Word are two factors that will help us hear what He is saying to us.

How much time do we spend reading and studying God's Word? Do we dig around in it only to find answers to our current questions, or are we opening ourselves to the Scriptures often and regularly? Mundane questions, perhaps. But let's not be too quick to dismiss them. Often what we *wish* were true is quite different from what *is* true. Even pastors and pastoral staff, in a recent survey, admitted that despite their intentions the only concentrated time they spent listening to God in the Scriptures was when they were preparing sermons or devotional material to use in their ministries.

But even *time spent* listening is not in itself any guarantee of hearing the voice of God. In the third chapter of his gospel, Mark records that some teachers of the law came from Jerusalem to observe Jesus and hear what He had to say. The primary responsibility of these men was to examine and copy the Scriptures. After listening and watching, they accused Jesus of being demon-possessed. The very ones who spent most of their time in the Scriptures were totally unable to recognize God's voice when they heard it. Study time in itself guarantees nothing.

When we come to God in His Word, we must bring believing hearts. We are listening to the living communication of a powerful and loving God with His needy people. Could His words possibly be insensitive to *who* we are and *where* we are? Martha as much as accused Christ of not caring about her plight! No wonder she wasn't listening to Him. She unconsciously doubted His good intentions toward her.

When we believe that God lovingly seeks our best and that He is vastly more sensitive to us than we are to ourselves, we will *seek* to hear Him. When we doubt God's intentions, His intimate caring, or His ability to speak directly to us and work powerfully in our lives, we may go through the motions of Bible reading, but we won't be listening expectantly to God. We will relegate God's thoughts to the "spiritual" part of our lives, while we live out our days in the remaining realms.

All of life is spiritual. Christ is *in* us! God wants to teach us how to please Him in every aspect of the chaos of reality. To this end He speaks to us clearly when we take time to listen believingly. He wants to bring all of who He is to bear on all of who we are. Believing God's loving intentions will express itself in part in a willingness to change. If I am closed to the idea of personal change in a particular area, I have plugged my spiritual ears with my fingers.

A friend of ours complained to his doctor of stomach pain and related symptoms. The doctor performed the usual tests and asked numerous questions. Based on our friend's answers, his manner, and the absence of any positive test results, the doctor concluded the pain was a direct result of stress. But our friend wasn't open to hear and act on the doctor's diagnosis. He had stopped listening early in the conversation and afterward put the whole thing out of his mind. When we asked him how it went, his simple conclusion was, "He told me it's all in my head. Shows you what he knows—it's my stomach that's killing me. Have to find a better doctor." His unwillingness to learn and make some changes in his lifestyle blocked his access to the truth. And he is the loser for it; he remains in constant discomfort.

When I hear what God is saying to me, it will most likely require that I change and grow. If my status quo is very comfortable, I will by all means resist change! But if I trust God in His loving character and His good intentions toward me, I will open myself to change, believing that He knows better than I do what is good for me and needed in my life.

The Book of Proverbs encourages us to hone our availability and attitude into an intense pursuit of what God has to say in His Word. We are not merely to be passively open and willing when God speaks, but we are to aggressively seek to know God's thoughts more and more. Solomon uses forceful words to describe the intensity of the seeking listener:

> My son, if you accept my words
>   and store up my commands within you,
> turning your ear to wisdom
>   and applying your heart to understanding,
> and if you call out for insight
>   and cry aloud for understanding,
> and if you look for it as for silver
>   and search for it as for hidden treasure,
> then you will understand the fear of the LORD
>   and find the knowledge of God.
> For the LORD gives wisdom,
>   and from his mouth come knowledge and
>   understanding. (Proverbs 2:1-6)

The Bible is our Master's voice. He uses His voice to teach us, rebuke us, correct us, and train us in righteousness (2 Timothy 3:16). He also uses it to delight us (Psalm 119:16), strengthen us (Psalm 119:28), and minister His love and comfort to us (Psalm 119:76). In the private time we spend with Him in His Word, with our hearts available and believing in His good intentions for our lives, we learn to hear and respond to our Almighty Master's voice.

Training our ears

We may believe that God uses His Word directly in our lives. We may trust His working with us. We may spend much time poring over our Bibles. Yet one more thing is needed if we are to know, when we come away from our time spent with God in His Word, that "God has spoken to me." To find out what this is, it will help to ask ourselves, "For what are we listening when we open our Bibles?" Perhaps you have had the experience, as I have, of wishing the words on the page would suddenly come alive. Yet you've once again been discouraged to find that despite your earnest intention, they remained simply printed words.

Why does this experience of lifelessness occur? Assuming we have dealt with any sin of which we are conscious (for sin surely deafens us more effectively than anything else), made ourselves available to God in His Word, and come trusting His Person, we must give our attention to the *focus* of our listening: *For what are we listening when we open our Bibles?*

Herein lies the root of our discouragement: We are listening for some*thing*, not some*one*. We are, as it were, trying to hear the *voice* of God, not the voice of *God*. This deviation of focus is subtle but pivotal. On it hinges our communication with our Lord, for it not only hinders our hearing, it also demotivates our praying. Who is excited about pouring his or her heart out to a God who seems silent? Without the right focus, listening degenerates to polite (if frustrated) attention, and praying becomes dry duty. What a common predicament this is among sincere Christians! Most of us would be hesitant to admit to such a condition—perhaps even to recognize it—but we need not be. God welcomes our admission and wants to shift our focus, to waken our ear "to listen like one being taught" (Isaiah 50:4).

See if you recognize any of these responses: "I'm not getting anything out of my quiet time (Bible study) lately"; "God isn't making Himself clear about what I should do"; "I keep asking God about my problem, but He hasn't given me any answers"; "I wish the Bible seemed more relevant to me—it's so dry and obscure most of the time."

Not one of these concerns is wrong, but all reflect the deviation of focus that is crucial here: These concerns are *issue*-centered, not *God*-centered. They focus on *what* God is saying, without a prior focus on *God Himself*.

Issue-centered listening is a perilous endeavor. By nature it is both selective and pressured. Often what results from such listening is a misuse of Scripture, an attempt to use one verse as a simple answer to a complex situation, an effort to justify selfish preference with Bible quotes, or a frantic grasping of a few words as a direct cue from God in a situation we want to resolve quickly.

This kind of listening commits the sin of treating God as a *means*, not an *end*. With such a frame of mind, whether we realize it or not, we are using God to try to get what we think we need. Instead, God calls us to listen to *Him*, to seek *His face*; He will take care of our needs. Matthew 6:33 echoes that very call: "But seek first his kingdom and his righteousness, and all these things will be given to you as well."

Our primary focus in listening must be God Himself. We must listen primarily for a Person—*the* Person—not a voice, a word, or a relevant truth. I say *primarily*, because although hearing God's voice and Word on relevant issues is an indispensable prerequisite to obedience, unless we are listening for God Himself, it is highly unlikely that His voice will ever be distinguished from the clamor around us.

And so, as we open the Word, our hearts should cry out with David, "Your face, LORD, I will seek" (Psalm 27:8). We can devise questions that will help keep this focus: What is revealed about *God* in these verses? What do I see of *God's* heart, thoughts, plans, intentions, character, work among men in this passage? How is *God* responding in this event or circumstance?

When we seek *God* in His Word, we will find ourselves hearing Him. We will know Him better and better and, in that context, the truths He reveals, the principles He shares, the insights He gives will become profoundly meaningful to our everyday existence. To seek truths and insights without a focus on God Himself is not to commune with a Person who will speak to us, but to collect ideas that will be at best temporarily helpful, at worst obscure and irrelevant. As we look into the *face* of God, the *words* God has for us will take on the perspective He intends for our current situation.

How does this work out practically? In Job's

trauma-laden life we see this shift of focus enacted in painful reality. Job is a believer. He prays and follows God. But when tragedy strikes like the staccato rounds of a machine gun, he searches vainly for an explanation. He cannot hear God. And what he believes about God, though true, certainly doesn't help him much. His friends heap more advice and information on him, which only makes matters worse. Job still does not hear God.

Then, thirty-eight chapters into Job's excruciating torment, God speaks. The Lord reveals Himself to Job, exposing His character, His heart, His thoughts, His ways with men. For the first time, Job shifts his eyes from what has happened to him to look fully at his God. Job is no longer listening for an answer, an explanation, a statement of just how God relates to the mess in which he agonizes. Now he is listening to God. He is no longer the bewildered sheep, stumbling about in search of the path, fearful and despairing. Now he is the weary, humbled, and comforted sheep, gratefully enraptured at the sight of his Shepherd's face as he describes the change of focus he has undergone: "My ears had heard of you but now *my eyes have seen you*" (Job 42:5).

Our private training takes place in the presence of God, through the *Word* of God. It is here that we learn to hear the voice of God as we keep our eyes on His Person. With our focus on Him, our minds willing and our ears open to hear His loving voice—even if it directs us to painful change—we will be taught by God's Spirit. In this context, God will direct His living Word to our need and understanding. Our minds will grasp the ways in which God's Word relates to the current concerns of our lives, and we will sense His specific instruction. Isaiah reminds us that "whether you turn to the right or to the left, your ears will hear a voice behind you, saying, 'This is the way; walk in it'" (Isaiah 30:21). Then, in excited surprise, we will exclaim, "God has spoken to me!"

Hearing His voice

There are basically two arenas in which we listen to God. One is the quiet, private times with God in His Word. Like the big, brown dog that had been trained to respond, we learn to recognize the Master's voice when we're alone with the Master. As Christians, we do well to develop patterns and habits that keep us available to God in His Word. We also must *pray* concerning our focus in those times and *think* about helpful ways to keep our eyes on God as we examine His Word. Among other helpful things, I have a Bible bookmark on which I inscribed Psalm 141:8—"But my eyes are fixed on You, O Sovereign LORD."

As we know our God more intimately, we will hear His voice more clearly, more specifically, more frequently. A.W. Tozer has written, "I think a new world will arise out of the religious mists when we approach our Bible with the idea that it is not only a book which was once spoken, but a book which is *now speaking*."[1]

The second arena in which we hear the voice of God is out in our "field." Only a small proportion of our time is spent in private involvement

with God in His Word. We can extend this involvement as we memorize verses and think about
them, listen to Bible tapes, and so on. But still, the
proportion will be small, relative to time spent on
other things.

Does God speak, then, only when our Bibles
are open, and remain silent when they are closed
and put back on the shelf? Must we glean all we
can of God in our private devotions, then step out
into the bright and noisy world hoping we "got"
enough to last us all day? God forbid! By such
thinking we will train ourselves in spiritual medi-
ocrity, because it encourages neither our Godward
focus in private nor our Godward receptivity in
public. For indeed, God is everywhere, seeking
always and without ceasing to communicate Himself to us. He will bring to mind the truths He has
shared with us in private, and through circumstances and people we will hear the echo of the
Voice we hear directly in His Word.

Much of what happens in our lives is God's
non-verbal communication with us. Do we find
ourselves thrown about by a series of unexpected
events? Perhaps God is saying, "Trust me." Are
we hurt and disappointed that plans or relationships haven't materialized in the way we had
hoped? It may be that God is telling us that He
alone is our security. Have we watched people's
lives turn about as they choose to obey God?
Maybe He is helping us observe how pleased He is
with obedience. The writer of Proverbs learned
such lessons from God by observation: "I applied
my heart to what I observed and learned a lesson

from what I saw" (Proverbs 24:32).

Perhaps we have a friend who faithfully advises us when we lose our objectivity. Or an acquaintance who criticizes us. Maybe we are just listening as someone tells about his spiritual journey, or how God dealt with him in a certain situation. In all these circumstances and many others, we find ourselves out in the "field" surrounded by voices, noise, and activity. If we have trained our ears to hear *God*, we will recognize His voice even in the most unlikely places.

When Abigail rode her donkey into a lonely mountain ravine, she found the man she sought. Slipping from her animal, she bowed down with her face to the ground, deliberately humbling herself before David, whom she feared and respected. Then from the lips of this woman came a stern but gracious warning, with a plea to forgive her ignorant and wicked husband, Nabal. David did not interrupt her. When she finished speaking, he responded, "Praise be to the LORD, the God of Israel, who has sent you today to meet me" (1 Samuel 25:32). David recognized the voice of his Master in Abigail's message because he knew God. He had become receptive to the God of all life. Even during his sword-brandishing, angry, and determined journey to attack Nabal and his men, David heard when God spoke.

Any voice we recognize as God's in the field of life must be the same voice we hear in the Bible. If we haven't cultivated our familiarity with God's powerfully comforting voice behind closed doors, we are in danger of mistaking many field voices as

God's. Much of what we hear, even in our Christian circles, sounds good, but it does not come from God. Or, even though it reflects God's truth, it may not be God's timely instruction for *us*. We can tie ourselves in knots when, because we do not hear *God*, we try to follow all the right-sounding voices, all the ones that claim God's direction.

Our ability to hear God's voice is a gift from Him that must be cultivated in private with a focus on God in His Word, and practiced everywhere.

The purpose of listening

God doesn't speak just to be heard. Nor does He reveal Himself only to be observed. He speaks, He reveals Himself, and He trains us to listen, so that we can live out His words and reflect His Person. Our hearing is meant to culminate in obedience. This is the nature of the Shepherd-sheep relationship that Jesus used when He spoke of our recognizing His voice.

Sheep are trained to know only one shepherd and his call. Without his direction they are hapless and helpless, bringing trouble and confusion upon themselves and any other sheep who might follow them. But when they hear and follow the voice of their shepherd, they are safe, nourished, and secure. The shepherd's voice is their axis of existence; everything revolves around it. If they stray out of earshot or stubbornly go their own way, death almost certainly awaits them.

How sheeplike we are! Let's commit ourselves to listening to our Shepherd and following His voice. As we train ourselves under the tutelage of God's Spirit to hear and obey His voice, we'll rejoice with David in the knowledge of His loving presence:

> The LORD is my shepherd, I shall lack nothing.
>   He makes me lie down in green pastures,
> he leads me beside quiet waters,
>   he restores my soul.
> He guides me in paths of righteousness
>   for his name's sake.
> Even though I walk
>   through the valley of the shadow of death,
> I will fear no evil,
>   for you are with me;
> your rod and your staff,
>   they comfort me.
> You prepare a table before me
>   in the presence of my enemies.
> You anoint my head with oil;
>   my cup overflows.
> Surely goodness and love will follow me
>   all the days of my life,
> and I will dwell in the house of the LORD
>   forever. (Psalm 23)

Notes

1. A.W. Tozer, *The Pursuit of God* (Harrisburg, Pennsylvania: Christian Publications, Inc., 1948), page 82.

6
Under the Gaze of God: Understanding His Scrutiny

Nathan's hunger cries pierced the night, waking us out of a sound sleep. I got up to feed our infant son, and my husband, Brian, chose to stay up with me. After the baby had quieted down, his immediate needs met, we sat side by side on the couch and gazed in quiet amazement at this week-old bundle of life that was our first-born child. His tiny arms criss-crossed his tummy; his little mouth made sucking movements in his sleep. I could feel the heat of his body right through his blue flannelette blanket as he lay in my lap.

The night was silent, the room was softly lit, and our thoughts drifted into wonder about the future. What would he be like—this Nathan—as a boy, as a man? What color hair would he have?

What would be his interests? What kind of personality would he develop? We became keenly aware that God had planned a little boy, a teenager, a man in this baby. And in a real sense, Nathan would spend the rest of his life becoming what he already was in the sight of God.

God has not ordained perpetual physical infancy; His design for life is growth. Each of us has within us the genetic design that determines both our potential and our limits. Our *limits* are often painfully clear; for example, a person may stop growing long before he or she reaches a desired size or shape. By contrast, our *potential* is often not so clear. It is, in fact, far greater than most of us imagine or even care to develop. Fortunate indeed is the child whose loving parents watch him faithfully in order to help him both live with his limits and develop his potential.

We have such a Parent: God our Father brings us into His family when we commit our lives, with faith and repentance, to Christ. Regardless of our chronological age, religious background, or personal maturity, we arrive in God's family as babies, spiritually speaking. But God does not intend perpetual spiritual infancy any more than He intends perpetual physical infancy. His design for spiritual life, as for physical life, is growth. Colossians 1:10 describes this God-designed growth: "And we pray this in order that you may live a life worthy of the Lord and may please him in every way: bearing fruit in every good work, growing in the knowledge of God."

As our loving Parent, our Father watches

over us faithfully in order to help us become who we already are—individuals conformed to the likeness of Christ. Paul declared in Romans 8:29, "For those God foreknew he also predestined to be conformed to the likeness of his Son, that he might be the firstborn among many brothers."

When we entered life in Christ, Jesus became for us "wisdom from God—that is, our righteousness, holiness and redemption" (1 Corinthians 1:30). God attributes Jesus' righteousness to us and considers us, therefore, to be already like Jesus. This is what theologians call "positional truth," and it means that our *standing* before God is just the same as Jesus' standing. Even as spiritual infants, we have the fullness of Christ within us.

God has designed our physical and spiritual lives similarly. In neither case, experientially, do we start out to be mature in who we are. Nathan couldn't walk, talk, or even focus his eyes as he lay in my lap at one week old. Many years later, he has still only partially become who he really is. Probably even a long and full life will not afford him sufficient time and opportunities to fulfill his potential in every respect.

In our spiritual life as well, we grow slowly from the stage of immaturity to maturity, increasingly gaining resemblance to the Christ whose likeness we already bear. As we grow and are built up, we gradually leave our vulnerable spiritual childhood to move into a mature likeness of Christ. Paul highlights this process in Ephesians 4:13-15:

> We [will] all reach unity in the faith and in the
> knowledge of the Son of God and become
> mature, attaining to the whole measure of the
> fullness of Christ. Then we will no longer be
> infants, tossed back and forth by the waves, and
> blown here and there by every wind of teaching
> and by the cunning and craftiness of men in their
> deceitful scheming. Instead, speaking the truth
> in love, we will in all things grow up into him
> who is the Head, that is, Christ.

We grow as we run the race of obedience with our eyes fixed on Jesus. Although we'll never be fully like Christ in this life, we will finally reach that goal when we cross over into eternity. In the meantime, God our Father watches over our development. He searches and examines us (Jeremiah 17:10). But He doesn't search and examine us in order to find out anything; He already knows all about us. His purpose is, rather, to reveal reality to us in order to clear away our misperceptions and replace them with His truth.

God longs to see us live according to His truth—about Him, about us, about the world around us. Those of us who are parents can at least in part identify with God's longing. When a teenage son agonizes over his awkwardness, we wish he could only realize how soon it will pass; for him, the wait seems like forever. If a child of ours is unduly influenced by unwholesome friendships, we try desperately to communicate to him or her where such relationships lead. When a lovely daughter is convinced she is ugly because someone at school made fun of her, we yearn for her to know the truth and be lifted above the taunts or criticisms of her peers.

God sees us, His growing children, in such a context. We have the likeness of Christ, but it is enveloped in our fallen nature. We are prone not only to sin, but to poor perspectives, inaccurate perceptions, and cloudy vision. We cannot know even our own heart because our insight is so obscured. In our efforts to evaluate ourselves, we often use all the wrong criteria: We compare ourselves with others. . . . Or we measure ourselves against our own expectations. . . . Or we look at ourselves in the light of what we think God wants from a "good Christian." . . . Or we allow current Christian fads to dictate the force and direction of our thinking.

All such examinations lead us to false conclusions. Like the awkward teenager, we agonize over superficial concerns while leaving essential heart issues untouched. We struggle in the darkness of our misperceptions, in a real sense enslaved to the labels we grasp: a success, a failure; spiritual, carnal; victorious, defeated.

God is committed to setting us free from such darkness by telling us the truth. Paul instructed the Romans to think of themselves "with sober judgment" (Romans 12:3). This instruction followed his directive to refuse to conform to the world's patterns and to let God renew their minds. Such mind renewal and sober judgment are the result of reflecting on God and ourselves in the light of the truth He reveals.

Far from being a fearful experience, this search of God over our lives is meant to bring accurate perspective, clear perception, and specific direction. As our Father, God has only one purpose: that we increasingly become who we already are in Christ. His intention is to build us up, not to tear us down. He wants to encourage us, not discourage us. And where change is needed, He promotes repentance and positive action, not entrapment in debilitating guilt. When we come to understand this intention of God's, and when we see the needless struggle as we sway this way and that depending on our current "measuring stick," we will welcome God's scrutiny as the pathway to freedom. Jesus assured those who believed in Him, "You will know the truth, and the truth will set you free" (John 8:32).

The light of God's Word

One group of words translated in the Scriptures as "examine" or "search" comes from a Hebrew root word meaning "to penetrate." This is the word used in Jeremiah 17:10—"I the LORD search the heart." God accomplishes this penetrating search of our heart with the light of His Word. Psalm 119:130 tells us, "The entrance of your words gives light." Nothing is hidden from the light of God, and He uses His Word as the vehicle of His light when He searches our heart. Hebrews describes the power of God's Word as it examines us:

> The word of God is living and active. Sharper than any double-edged sword, it penetrates even

to dividing soul and spirit, joints and marrow; it judges the thoughts and attitudes of the heart. Nothing in all creation is hidden from God's sight. Everything is uncovered and laid bare before the eyes of him to whom we must give account. (Hebrews 4:12-13)

When we read, study, think about, or even simply hear God's Word, and we are *listening* to Him, He will line up our life alongside His Word to reveal our progress in becoming like Christ. Together we will see both advances and needs. As Hebrews 4 indicates, God will deal with the very depths of our hearts as He shines the penetrating light of His Word in where no human eye can see, where we ourselves are not accustomed to looking. In this intimate search, God reveals both Himself and ourselves to us. We know Him better as He opens the depths of His Word to our listening hearts, and we see more of ourselves from God's viewpoint when He addresses Himself to areas of our lives. Without the light of God's Word, we don't have a truthful perception of ourselves, a proper perspective on our situation, or a clear direction for the next step in following Him.

Imagine yourself in an utterly dark room. You cannot identify its size, shape, contents, or your place in it. You can feel various objects around you, but they are fearfully suspect because you can't quite figure out what they are. You resist moving because you can't see where you're going. Panic mounts, and soon you cry for escape.

The prophet Elijah found himself in such a

dark room at a crisis point in his life. In 1 Kings 19 we read about a dramatic demonstration of the power of God, through which Elijah had made the false gods into a laughingstock. As a result, he was being threatened with revenge by Jezebel, King Ahab's wife. Elijah's perspective dissolved, true perception was hidden from him, and he lacked all sense of direction. He ran to the desert and, full of panic and desperation, asked God to take his life. In his darkness he saw neither himself nor his situation from God's perspective. Elijah's despair was reaching fatal proportions.

But God prepared Elijah to hear Him. How surprised Elijah must have been to discover that God did not thunder at him in the wind or shake him up with a rebuke in the earthquake or burn him with hot words in the fire! Certainly Elijah was in a frame of mind easily convinced of God's displeasure.

Instead, God turned on the lights. As He spoke quietly to the prophet, God gave Elijah truth about himself (he was not alone after all; seven thousand Israelites did not worship Baal) and perspective about his situation (the victory would continue; Jezebel's threat would not materialize). But God also gave Elijah an assignment, a *next step* in the process of what God was doing. The prophet was to go right back where he came from, anoint two new kings, and appoint Elisha as his successor. Elijah was freed from the tyranny of his darkness by a word from God. His gentle voice went straight to Elijah's heart and put him back on course.

When you and I listen to God, we learn the truth about ourselves. We can then arrive at a sober judgment, a true picture. The searchlight of God's Word may illuminate an attitude or behavior pattern, perhaps a relationship or a decision-making direction. In the circle of illumination, we begin our own search: Why am I in this situation? Does it affect anyone? Who needs to be forgiven? What needs to be corrected? Was I needlessly fearful of something? What is my goal in this? Does my goal match God's goal? How can I use this gift or opportunity? What does God want me to do next?

Such a process is invigorating because God is building us up through it. The results are hope and progress and a deeper intimacy with the One who has spoken truth to us. It also results in greater obedience, as David indicates in Psalm 119:59: "I have considered my ways and have turned my steps to your statutes."

Contrast this positive effect to the downward spiral we create with negative introspection. We may begin our search where God has not shone His light. Or perhaps we react despondently when God reveals truth about us. We make matters worse by interrogating rather than investigating. We ask ourselves, How could I be so stupid? Can't I ever change? Why am I such a failure? Our efforts result in despair, and, like Elijah, we give in to hopelessness.

Equally dangerous is any examination we carry out based solely on our own or others' standards. For example, as we look at all the responsibilities we carry, or how many people we've helped, or all the wonderful comments people make about us, we become perilously satisfied with ourselves. Such false satisfaction breeds the same problem as negative introspection; since we are not listening to God's evaluation, we are not walking in truth. Many of us swing regularly from excited self-satisfaction to dejected self-incrimination. As a result, we are not stepping forward by God's direction. Rather, the motion in our lives is side to side, like a pendulum.

If we welcome God's scrutiny as He shines the light of His Word into our lives, and if we fully face the truth He reveals, we'll find ourselves growing more clearheaded, more determined to live for Him, and more strengthened for the next step of the journey.

The fires of life

Peter wept uncontrollably as he leaned against the mud brick wall outside the courtyard. The pre-dawn darkness wrapped itself around him, sending its chill deep into his stomach. His hope of an imminent kingdom, his expectations of Jesus, and—most gripping—his estimate of himself had all been smashed. He was a broken man, a man who had just discovered his own faithlessness. He had denied Christ.

Three people had questioned Peter's association with Christ. The hour of their questioning had become for Peter a test of fire. When it was over, only the truth remained. He had thought he was bold and strong; actually, he was weak and fearful. About two months later Peter underwent a similar test. While preaching about Christ to the people of Jerusalem, he and John were seized and dragged off to prison. Did the Peter who escaped one threatening situation by denying Christ again recant in order to protect himself? Far from it! Instead, filled with the Holy Spirit and with courage, he boldly preached Christ to his captors.

What had happened to Peter in that two-month interval? He had accepted the truth revealed about himself and faced the risen Christ in new humility. No longer self-assured, he allowed Christ to challenge him and the Holy Spirit to prepare him for a phenomenal ministry.

Jesus had predicted Peter's failure, but Peter had refused to believe Him (Matthew 26: 31-35). Peter was so oblivious to the truth that only hard evidence could make him face it. God often uses our circumstances as a vehicle to reveal His truth. He wants us to come face to face with reality, and sometimes experience is the best mirror. I was thoroughly convinced that I was a patient person— until I had children. It didn't take long for me to face the fact of my real nature in the test of experience!

The Hebrew root word that we translate as "observes" and "examines" in Psalm 11:4-5 means "tests" or "proves": "He observes the sons of men. . . . The LORD examines the righteous." This is the same word David uses in Psalm 26:2 and in Psalm 139:23 when he invites God to test and search him. The fires of life—its trials, its choices, its challenges—are from God. He uses them as a proving ground. And for those who are open to God's observations, they become valuable mirrors of truth.

Yet we fear this proving ground, because we are prone to think that God will always show us our shortcomings, and too much of that is difficult for anyone to take. Certainly our shortcomings will become visible, but they are not the focus of God's purpose. Our testing in the experience of life bears the mark of God's supreme intention: the revelation and honor of Christ in our lives. Peter explains in 1 Peter 1:7 that "these [trials] have come so that your faith—of greater worth than gold, which perishes even though refined by fire—may be proved genuine and may result in praise, glory and honor when Jesus Christ is revealed."

As we go through circumstances of fire, God searches through our mixed bag of reactions to find the nugget of faith—however small it may be—that He can hold up to let it draw praise to Christ and demonstrate, at least in part, our resemblance to Him. And as our loving Father, He will use the same opportunity to show us how we might grow to resemble Christ even more.

Some years ago a friend of ours faced an extremely unpleasant encounter with his family, who made no effort to hide their disapproval of his commitment to Christ. He was anxious and fearful as the weekend visit approached, convinced that his faith would not withstand their attack. By Friday, his dejected countenance clearly showed his desire to avoid the entire incident.

Then Monday morning arrived, and the

phone rang. Our friend's voice was cheery and encouraged as his story unfolded. The weekend had indeed been unpleasant, and many derogatory comments had left him emotionally bruised. But God had revealed to him that his faith was greater than he had imagined. In the midst of his family's harangue he had been able to rely on God and remember key verses, with which God strengthened him. He had even found his usually angry response tempered and a new compassion emerging. The refining fire had revealed a gold nugget of faith and stimulated a new song of praise.

However, during this testing experience our friend also became acutely aware of some deep needs in his life: to concretely demonstrate more caring to his family, to listen carefully rather than be quick to defend himself, and so on. But seeing these needs was not discouraging, because they were specific and part of his progress toward the goal of knowing and becoming like Christ. He had already begun to act on his new insight, and, profiting from the revealing effects of God's testing, was moving ahead.

None of us has "arrived," or ever will, in this life. Time will see us, as God's children, continually becoming what He has already created us to be. As we avoid the traps of unhealthy introspection and comparison, and honestly search our own hearts in the light of God's revealed truth through His Word and our everyday circumstances, we can rejoice; we have that much clearer an understanding of how to reach our goal: knowing and becoming like Christ.

Paul had this long-range perspective. He wasn't frustrated by his journey or disheartened because he hadn't yet "arrived." Instead, he allowed his desire to know and be like Christ to so impassion him that he could welcome as friends any circumstances, painful or otherwise, that could take him closer to his goal. He used all of life to help him "press on":

> Not that I have already obtained all this, or have already been made perfect, but I press on to take hold of that for which Christ Jesus took hold of me. Brothers, I do not consider myself yet to have taken hold of it. But one thing I do: Forgetting what is behind and straining toward what is ahead, I press on toward the goal to win the prize for which God has called me heavenward in Christ Jesus. (Philippians 3:12-14)

God is watching you today, and He is watching me. He wants to reveal reality to us—His truth—so that we might press on in our loving, knowing, and becoming like Jesus Christ. As His Word examines us and His fire tests us, He prompts us to search our own hearts in the light of His revelation. And as we apply this truth that God reveals, we *grow up* in Him.

A young pianist was preparing for a session with a world-renowned master, a man he greatly respected and tried to emulate. The famous master musician was to spend several days with this promising pianist, examining, evaluating, and advising him. Friends of the young man asked him if he was anxious about what promised to be such an intense and profound scrutiny by this famous performer. "Oh no!" he answered. "I look forward to it with great longing, for *he will only help me to become more like him!*"

7
Let Us Run Our Race: Choosing to Obey

Nehemiah shielded his eyes from the late afternoon sun as he looked out over the colorful crowd. Most of the people were gathering up their things, moving quickly and excitedly in anticipation of an evening of unexpected celebration. But not everyone was joyful. From where he stood, Nehemiah could see Jeshua and Hanun calming two older men whose weeping had gone on long after others had focused themselves on the sacred sweetness of this significant day. Elsewhere among the crowd, other Levites, too, comforted mourning men and women, calming them and sending them on their way.

The square at the Water Gate finally emptied, and Nehemiah paused in the new quietness of this dedication day to thank God for the power-ful work He had begun in this band of Israelite refugees who had resettled Jerusalem and rebuilt its walls. Deep joy gripped him—he hadn't known such joy since the day King Artaxerxes had released him from service to return here.

Nehemiah thanked God for Ezra, whose careful reading of the Book of the Law of Moses had flowed to the people like a rush of cool water over hot, dry land. He thanked God for the Levites, whose instruction among the Israelites helped to draw Ezra's readings into relevant focus. And he thanked God for the people, whose sensi-tive hearts had been struck by the contrast between God's commands and their own lives.

Almost without exception, the hearers had become mourners, and many had grieved aloud as they realized their sinful condition before God. Nehemiah and the Levites had to draw the people's attention off their grief to the awesome sacredness of God's new work among them. It was a cause for great rejoicing that the people had heard, understood, and responded to God's Word, and so the evening would be set aside for celebration.

"Go and enjoy choice food and sweet drinks," Nehemiah had told the people, "and send some to those who have nothing prepared. This day is sacred to our LORD. Do not grieve, for the joy of the LORD is your strength" (Nehemiah 8:10). The sounds of music began to fill the evening air. Nehemiah praised God once more, then left the square to join the joyful celebration.

Early the next morning, a smaller group gathered around Ezra. The family heads, the priests, and the Levites all settled themselves again to hear what was written in God's Book. The words were not only specific, but timely. The Law included instructions for a week-long Feast of Tabernacles to begin on the fifteenth day of the seventh month. During this feast-week the people were to live in booths made of branches, and on the eighth day they were to hold an assembly (Leviticus 23:33-43).

The men who had gathered around Ezra looked at one another. No one voiced what they all knew: Today was already the second day of the seventh month. Now they had only thirteen days to get the people ready to once again make spiritual history in obedience to God. Centuries had passed since God's people had last celebrated the Feast of Tabernacles.

Ezra gave some instructions to ensure that each man present would share the proclamation among a given group of Israelites. Together they would make certain everyone heard the plan: "Go out into the hill country and bring back branches from olive and wild olive trees, and from myrtles, palms and shade trees, to make booths" (Nehemiah 8:15).

The next thirteen days were devoted to the unusual project of building branch-booths. Roofs, courtyards, and open areas near the Temple sprung up in little stick houses. Anticipation and excitement were almost tangible among the people as the fifteenth day of the month drew near.

On the morning of the fifteenth day, Nehemiah awoke with an overpowering awareness of the day's significance. Today God's wandering and wayward people would realign themselves with the design God had created for them. Months of labor, leading, and fighting opposition had taken their toll on Nehemiah, but this morning his weariness seemed to roll away in the renewal of what God was doing.

Nehemiah had known that rebuilding Jerusalem's walls, although a great and spiritually meaningful accomplishment, would be a hollow victory without personal revival among the Israelites. Today marked the greater milestone: God's people responding to God's Word in obedient submission to God's Person and plan. That He would again woo and be gracious to His fickle people struck awe in Nehemiah's heart. This was indeed a sacred day.

And what a day it was! Nehemiah had never seen such joy among these people. Even the completion of the wall had not produced the jubilance that he could see and hear and feel as he walked among the booths and observed the people. "From the days of Joshua son of Nun until that day, the Israelites had not celebrated it like this. *And their joy was very great*" (Nehemiah 8:17, italics added).

+   +   +

So we see that in the fifth century B.C., a remnant of God's people gathered in the partially rebuilt city of Jerusalem and listened to Him. As they came to an understanding of what His Word was saying, they sensed God's scrutiny upon their lives. And when they looked at themselves from this new perspective, they broke down and wept because of what they saw.

The Israelites heard the Word of God and responded from their hearts. But they went way beyond a heart response. When they heard specific instruction from the Law regarding their immediate future (the building of booths and the celebration of the Feast of Tabernacles), they had a pivotal choice to make. Three options faced them: First, they could relegate God's instruction to relevance only for another time and place, and set it aside. Second, they could postpone action to the following year, citing their inexperience, the short preparation time available, and the accomplishments for God already made that year. Third, they could enter wholeheartedly into actively carrying out the expressed will of God. By the grace of God, they chose to obey immediately.

We have this same God who, by His grace, has freed us to choose obedience (see Romans 8:2-4). And the progression in making our choice is much the same as it was for the Israelites of Nehemiah's day: listening to God; responding from our heart as God examines and tests us; acknowledging our condition as God reveals it to us through a combination of His Word and His work in our life; and resolving to obey Him with fresh commitment and determination, and often with emotion.

But what happens next? How can we translate commitment into action? The Israelite Christians to whom the Apostle James wrote around 45 A.D. were apparently facing the same choice that the Israelite remnant in Jerusalem had faced five centuries earlier: how to handle God's instruction. Knowing the significance of the choice, James wrote:

> Do not merely listen to the word, and so deceive yourselves. Do what it says. Anyone who listens to the word but does not do what it says is like a man who looks at his face in a mirror and, after looking at himself, goes away and immediately forgets what he looks like. But the man who looks intently into the perfect law that gives freedom, and continues to do this, not forgetting what he has heard, but doing it—he will be blessed in what he does. (James 1:22-25)

You and I face this choice daily. God continually challenges us to act on our commitment. In fact, He says if our faith commitment remains inactive, it is dead; it is no commitment at all. What will we do with God's instruction? How will we build into our lives the active demonstration of commitment through obedience? How will we handle what God has shown us?

The Israelite remnant in Jerusalem handled God's instruction effectively. And the result was not only a significant step of national and individual obedience, but also a source of *very great joy*, the joy that uniquely belongs to pleasing God. We can learn from Nehemiah's band how to carry out the commitment we express with our lips.

Focus on God and His Word

Nehemiah 8:1-8 reveals to contemporary readers a surprising fact: While Ezra read aloud from the Book of the Law, the people *stood* from daybreak until noon, listening "attentively." And following that stretch of endurance they eagerly absorbed Levitical instruction that helped them, in their Babylonian mindset, understand the Hebrew meaning. (Many of us get impatient after half an hour of listening to the Word, and usually we're *sitting*.)

Through the Word, they saw God. It was this encounter with their Lord, making them painfully aware of the gap between God's laws and their lives, that moved them to a genuine heart response.

As we listen attentively to God, He will stir our inner life as well. Under His scrutiny, issues will surface, and we'll find our character revealed. We will become aware of how He views us, and we will grow in our desire to please Him.

But what is the next step in rekindling our commitment?

Face the truth

The labor-weary Israelites inside Jerusalem's newly restored walls were still under Babylonian rule because for dozens of generations—including their own—God's people had been faithless. Their monumental prayer of confession, recorded in Nehemiah 9, indicates they were fully aware of their guilt. Facing that truth brought them to tears. Like the prodigal son who came to his senses in a pig sty, the Israelites finally realized how distant they were from the Father and how much their predicament was truly of their own making.

Facing the truth as God reveals it means taking personal responsibility for the condition of our lives. We cannot truly comprehend God's communication to us as long as we blame other people or circumstances for what is our fault.

A woman once came to us for counsel concerning the serious financial debt she was in. Although we didn't know her well, her comments revealed a fairly irresponsible attitude toward money in general and her own resources in particular. Her deepening debt jeopardized her ability to make decisions in other areas, and it had long since squeezed out generosity—yet she was still unwilling to face up to her responsibility. She perceived herself as a victim—of her father's financial tactics, the unsteady economy, the demands of others, even the government. Although all these factors were undeniably involved, the crucial issue was her willingness to see her responsibility for the situation as it was and deal with it accordingly.

Weeks later, this woman finally came to the difficult point of taking her eyes off what others had done. She paid attention to what God was saying to *her*, specifically through the principle that Paul establishes in Romans 13:7. Her unwillingness to accept her responsibility had clouded her view of the truth. When she *did* accept responsibility, however, she began to understand and act on that truth.

Choosing to obey God involves focusing on

Him and His Word, and then facing the truth about ourselves and our need to change. The next step in the process of acting on our commitment is simple and practical: Find an opportunity to respond to God's instruction.

Find an opportunity

It wasn't hard for the men gathered with Ezra to realize that they were on the threshold of a critical opportunity to carry out the commands of God's Word. They knew exactly what should be done, and the time frame: thirteen days! Yet even with such clarity and urgency, their obedience was still their choice.

We walk constantly among opportunities to obey God. Perhaps for some of us, however, years have passed since we had to make an earth-shaking decision, and we feel that opportunities to obey are over. Nothing could be further from the truth! We are immersed in opportunities to please God, but most of the time we don't even recognize them! Every relationship, activity, response, thought, attitude, and circumstance has potential for obedience. Remember this key principle: *Change is possible only if we are willing to find an opportunity to take the first step*—a step of obedience, a specific application of God's truth.

Let's imagine that God's scrutiny of us has revealed an aspect of character that needs to be brought into greater conformity with the character of Christ within us. For example, as soon as things don't fit into our timing, we lose patience— which leads to other problems. But the root cause is our impatient response.

How can we change such a built-in pattern? The same way we developed it—one opportunity at a time. Having faced this issue squarely, we can now identify an opportunity to replace impatience with patience. Daily interaction with a slow co-worker, for example, would provide first-rate practice in this area. Our focus would now turn to how to take advantage of this opportunity in an obedient response to God's prompting.

Follow a plan

"The plans of the diligent lead to profit," according to Proverbs 21:5. Certainly this principle couldn't be more appropriate than when applied to planning in order to obey God!

The Israelite remnant of Nehemiah's time had a plan; God had given them one. They knew that the first step was collecting branches, the second was building booths, and so on. Most of the time, however, God does not do our planning for us. His willingness to give specific plans to many leaders in the Old Testament is an indication of the importance He places on thinking responsibly about how to move out in obedience.

Obedience won't just happen; we must take care to carry out God's will. Peter emphasizes that such care requires "every effort" (2 Peter 1:5). A plan that helps us carry out our intended obedience is a significant part of pleasing God. (The next chapter will discuss in detail how we can take God's principles and create specific plans to help us obey His Word.) Following such a plan, however, does not guarantee that we will always see its immediate significance or results.

As the Israelites gathered in the square at the Water Gate and wept before God, they were overwhelmed by how far from Him they had fallen. It might have occurred to them that a ritual feast would make very little difference in their condition. What effect, realistically, could seven days of celebration have on lives trained in decades of neglect toward God?

It may seem simplistic to think that a small step in a limited opportunity can make any real difference in our deep-rooted needs or help to change whole areas of our lives. But God is concerned with the direction of our steps, not their size or number. Even when our obedience seems dwarfed by our need, it is material in the hands of God for His working. Our obedience doesn't change us; *God does*. What matters is whether or not we're doing what He says—not how significant or insignificant our act of obedience seems to us. God isn't bound by the size of what we have to offer (think of what Jesus did with five loaves of bread and two fishes), but He is concerned with our heart.

When, in a response to God from our heart, we move out in steps of obedience, we may find that changes occur far out of proportion to the steps we take. This wonder is evidence of God's work. He takes our "inch" of obedience and turns it into a "mile" of progress. When we look back at that mile stretching behind us, we can only thank God for His grace at work.

Nehemiah's band of Israelites found themselves in just this situation. In a matter of days their hearts and their lives moved "miles" in following God. Their choice to obey God—to seize the opportunity at hand, to follow the plan of pleasing God—was not the source of the change; *God* was. In His hands, their deliberate efforts to please Him were multiplied into a life-changing process.

And so it can be with us. Let us listen attentively to God, take to heart the result of His scrutiny, find an opportunity for application, and make a deliberate, planned effort to obey God's Word to us. What will be the results? Deep joy is one. A changed life is another. But a far greater result is that our very lives will become fragrant expressions of love to our God.

8
One Step at a Time: Practicing Obedience

The thirteen men had settled themselves around the table, and the evening meal was being served. Jesus looked at these men whom He loved fiercely. What a mixture of emotions welled up inside Him! He yearned to stay longer with His friends. He thought sadly of the devastation they would experience when He left them. With tenderness, He recalled how hard they tried to learn from Him, yet how little they really understood.

He would soon leave eleven of these twelve men to carry the reality of God's Kingdom into the rest of the world. They hardly seemed ready. In fact, their ongoing argument about which of them was the greatest had erupted again just moments before. Jesus knew they would be effective messengers only after they replaced their competitive spirits with love for one another.

There wasn't much time left. Jesus was keenly aware that the rest of His earthly life was now measured in hours. Yet He also knew that His disciples desperately needed one last lesson in love. He would invest much of His precious remaining time in teaching His men what it meant to love one another.

Jesus stood up. Conversation ceased and all eyes riveted on Him. These men knew that Jesus was the son of God, their Messiah. He had full authority to ask anything of them. Had He stood up to command their loyalty? Or to finally appoint one of them as the group's leader? Or perhaps this was His time to leave, as He had told them. They sensed something important was about to happen.

Jesus began to remove His outer clothing. Anticipation gave way to surprise, then to confusion, on the disciples' faces. Before they dared ask what He was doing, He had wrapped a towel around His waist, and was filling a basin with water.

Confusion turned to shame; they realized now that Jesus was going to do the job that none of them would stoop to—washing the dust of the road off the others' feet. Why didn't He just instruct one of the servants to do this? Their Master was behaving like their servant! Because of their pride, Jesus was left with the most degrading task.

Each man sensed his own loathing of the job Jesus chose to do. But He didn't seem to feel degraded at all. He didn't hurry to finish. He even

insisted, over Peter's objections, that it was need-
ful for Him to perform this act.

What would He say to them, they wondered,
when He finished? Would He rebuke them for
their pride? Humbled now, they were ready to
bear His words, and to take His teaching to heart.
The disciples watched in silence as Jesus emptied
out the water, dried His hands, put His clothing
back on, and sat down. But no rebuke was
forthcoming.

As Jesus looked around at them, meeting
their eyes one by one, He knew they would be
shocked by what He was about to say to them. He
also knew that whatever He impressed on their
readied hearts now would stay with them all their
lives.

> "Do you understand what I have done for you?"
> he asked them. "You call me 'Teacher' and
> 'Lord,' and rightly so, for that is what I am. Now
> that I, your Lord and Teacher, have washed your
> feet, you also should wash one another's feet. I
> have set you an example that you should do as I
> have done for you. I tell you the truth, no servant
> is greater than his master, nor is a messenger
> greater than the one who sent him." (John
> 13:12-16)

+ + +

With His hands, His basin, His towel, and
His words, Jesus had translated love for the disciples. He turned their understanding of love upside
down, then injected into their incredulity this

challenge: "Now that you know these things, you will be blessed if you do them" (John 13:17).

Jesus wanted to revolutionize the disciples' lives. He knew that if He had simply told them to "love one another," they would have understood little of how to carry out His command. So He showed them clearly: Love serves. Then He reinforced His example with His words. But Jesus also knew that these disciples would not change unless they began doing what they now had started to understand. So He challenged them to serve one another. Later in the evening He commanded them to love one another (John 13:34).

Jesus wanted them to both understand and act on what He had told them. As a result, they would change inwardly and outwardly; an altered attitude and perception would be demonstrated by a shift in behavior. Jesus, the Master Teacher, was showing them how to obey, and He was transforming them.

We, too, need to be transformed, in our behavior and character, our actions and attitudes, our outer life and inner life. These are inseparably linked, and the most effective plan for obedience will encourage both increased understanding and definite action. God will bring about permanent life changes as we respond in these aspects. And we will find both our character and our conduct being transformed.

Our understanding

In Ephesians 4:23 (AMP) Paul urges his readers to "be constantly renewed in the spirit of your mind—having a fresh mental and spiritual attitude." Our minds are renewed as we increasingly adopt perceptions, beliefs, attitudes, and knowledge consistent with God's character and His Word. Although our Christian environments (family, church, friends) will help us in this issue of mind-renewal, it is essentially a personal matter involving our willingness to think God's way, and our efforts to discover God's truth.

Have you submitted your mind to God? Are you *willing to think His way* about issues and areas of life as they surface? The disciples thought they were. But when Jesus began to show them His definition of love, which involved His own death and the servant nature of loving, they resisted Him. They resisted thinking God's way about a love and commitment even to the point of death. On at least one occasion Peter cried, "No, Lord!" when Jesus tried to help him understand truth.

We especially need to be willing to have God change our minds on the things about which we are the most sensitive. God has truth to give us, truth we must allow to infiltrate our attitudes and actions. His truth is highly relevant to where we are; it's not hidden on a theological shelf. Rather, God's truth speaks to our security, our worth, our purpose, our relationships, our freedom, our rights, our attitudes, our needs, our responsibilities, and so on.

Such willingness to change our thinking involves honesty. As we are willing to think God's way, to see things from *His* perspective, we'll need to honestly face what He says, both about us and about Himself. How easy it is to minimize the seriousness, or avoid the real nature, of an issue.

Such willingness also requires that we be specific. God doesn't deal with us in vague generalities. His teaching may be broad, but when the time comes to understand how that teaching relates to us, He is direct and specific. If we say, "I need to be more loving" or "I'd be wise to strengthen my gifts" or "I have an attitude problem," we fall short of the deep honesty and crucial clarity we need in order to express willingness to think God's way. The willingness God desires will be marked by honesty and specificity: "I need to serve my spouse's needs"; "I could practice my gift of helping by meeting needs in my neighborhood"; "I am resentful toward my teacher."

The disciples eventually came to the point where their willingness went beyond words and intention. They became willing to have God's perspective, facing it honestly and relating it specifically to their lives. This willingness was foundational to the transformation that the Jewish leaders observed in Peter and John: "When they saw the courage of Peter and John and realized that they were unschooled, ordinary men, they were astonished and they took note that these men had been with Jesus" (Acts 4:13).

So, then, mind-renewal first involves our daily *willingness* to let God teach us His perspective, so that it might become ours.

It also involves our efforts to learn that perspective. With our minds willing to think God's way, our investigation of Scripture becomes incredibly fruitful. Are you willing to accept whatever God shares, even if it's a rebuke? Then always remember His promise: "If you had responded to my rebuke, I would have poured out my heart to you and made my thoughts known to you" (Proverbs 1:23).

We need to find out what God says about whatever we are dealing with. This is particularly true today, because our minds are saturated with the world's perspective, whether we realize it or not. Furthermore, if we have been Christians a while, we've also absorbed a lot of secondhand information from various Christian sources, some of it extremely well-prepared from the Word, but some of it based on experience plus a shallow understanding of God's truth.

Specific searches in the Word of God can be brief or extensive. A good concordance is an invaluable help for doing a topical search. For instance, many character issues can be initially examined by tracing one word, such as patience, anger, truthfulness, or faithfulness, and variants of the word. In an extended study, or just meditating on a couple of verses daily for a week, you will discover some of what God says about a topic.

Many issues of life are the subjects of existing Bible studies. Bible dictionaries, topically arranged Bible reference works, and *The Treasury of Scripture Knowledge* would all be valuable helps as we work to learn the mind of God. A good general dictionary often provides amazing clarity as we read and study Scripture. It's provision of shades of meaning can give rich opportunity for mulling over the implications of what God is saying. Writing down what we find out helps to lodge our new understanding in our minds, as well as to make our insights available to share.

As we grow in discovering God's perspective from His Word, it's a wise idea to memorize a related verse or two to consolidate our understanding, and give God a tool in our hearts to pull His Word back into our focus when He needs to.

Books are also valuable resources in renewing our minds according to God's truth. Reading biblically-oriented books is one way of making the effort to learn God's thoughts. As a particular issue arises, our reading habit can be directed toward books that provide relevant, helpful, biblically sound information and insight.

Not every truth God shares needs further clarification or more study, but for those that do—and these will generally be the issues of character and patterns that are significant building blocks in our lives—we must be willing to adopt God's perspective and faithful to search it out. In this way we prepare for godly change—from the inside out. This is the transformation that Jesus offered His first disciples, and it is the same transformation He promises us today.

Our action

When God begins to show us some truth about Himself, ourselves, or how we relate to Him, others, and life in general, there will always be some action we can take to step out in obedience to that truth. This opportunity to actually live out, even in some small way, the commands of God is probably one of the most creative and exciting aspects of the Christian life! (Chuck Swindoll's book *Growing Strong in the Seasons of Life* is a rich source of creative ideas for practical obedience. I recommend it highly.) To literally *do* what God says, to put legs and feet to our understanding: This is what God has always intended for His people. Understanding is essential, yet in many cases, we already *understand* enough to keep us actively obeying for years to come!

Sometimes the action we need to take is obvious (if we are honest). For example, if we have deceived someone, Colossians 3:9 (which says, "Do not lie to each other") should lead us to confession and to making right the wrong. An honest willingness to hear God on these specific issues, plus a commitment to do what He says, will keep us acting on the Word daily. These one-time applications as we relate to people, make decisions, and so on, reflect choices that God will use as catalysts to the marvelous transformation He has undertaken in our lives.

This kind of application is based on an "as-you-go" principle. The floor in our house seems to act as a magnet for kleenex bits, rubber bands, tiny toys, pen tops, and pennies (among other things). I have tried to develop the habit of picking these things up "as I go." I'm trying to train our children to do the same. Many household and business routines are best accomplished on an as-you-go basis. Otherwise they pile up and create problems.

Choices to obey God as we go are specific ways to walk in the Spirit. Choosing to keep a promise, choosing to get understanding rather than react, choosing to serve rather than demand rights—these and a lifetime of choices are the specific obedience God commands in obeying Him as we go.

Other areas of obedience require far more attention than we can give them as we go. Major changes are sometimes needed, and these involve many steps and a fair stretch of time. Such changes can be either remedial (oriented to correction) or progressive (oriented to building and strengthening). In either case, God has given us the responsibility to develop a plan that will help to move us in the right direction.

Does such planning reflect legalism or a "sanctification-by-works" mentality? Only if our trust shifts from God to the plan. The most brilliant and spiritual plan could never accomplish anything in itself for the Kingdom of God. Only God transforms lives. Only God creates intimacy between creature and Creator. Only God renders effective our puny efforts to influence our world.

But He has chosen to give us a part in the process. That part is obedience. And He has given us example after example of how He expects His people to plan out their obedience. He expects us to think wisely, plan carefully, and work hard in obeying Him. Proverbs 14:22, blended with Ephesians 5:15, is a potent expression of God's desire in this regard: "But those who plan what is good find love and faithfulness. . . . Be very careful, then, how you live—not as unwise but as wise."

God has worked miracles through some rather unusual strategies! He told Gideon to defeat the Midianites. But first, using a series of interesting criteria, He reduced Gideon's resources from an army of 32,000 to a band of 300. Even so, He promised victory. What plan did Gideon devise for defeating the Midianites? A very creative one, to say the least! Gideon gave each man a trumpet, an empty jar, and a torch to put inside the jar. Then he divided his meager band in three groups. When the men carried out their orders on cue, a most unusual battle resulted:

> Gideon and the hundred men with him reached the edge of the camp at the beginning of the middle watch, just after they had changed the guard. They blew their trumpets and broke the jars that were in their hands. The three companies blew the trumpets and smashed the jars. Grasping the torches in their left hands and holding in their right hands the trumpets they were to blow, they shouted, "A sword for the LORD and for Gideon!" . . . When the three hundred trumpets sounded, the LORD caused the men throughout the camp to turn on each other with their swords. (Judges 7:19-20, 22)

God worked through Gideon's strategy and gave the victory! Plans to obey God, as described in Scripture, range from such off-beat strategies as Gideon's to the highly technical and precise plan for the building of Solomon's temple. God accomplishes His purpose through every plan that is designed with obedience in mind.

We can have fun planning our obedience. Certainly it's serious business, but God has given us room to enjoy it immensely and to be very creative as we plan to obey Him. Two questions will help to give birth to some strategic thinking as we focus, with God, on a needed change in an area of our lives: 1. What are its roots? 2. What are its fruits? Whether the change needed is remedial or progressive, these two questions will be useful.

1. *What are its roots?* If this area involves sinful behavior or attitudes, when do we first observe them? In what situation(s)? Under what conditions? What needs or desires prompt us in this direction?

Answering these and similar questions can help us identify the arena of temptation in which we are involved. Sin follows temptation. Sometimes that arena will be a physical situation (such as a bar); sometimes it will be a belief or assumption ("I have a right to be angry when that happens"). Identifying points of origin helps us see where our strategy should begin.

If, instead, the area has to do with progress, not correction, where does this new strength or pattern originate? What characteristics contribute to it? Under what conditions does it come into being? On what truths does it rest? Why is it important?

Responding to these questions will build conviction and motivation; it will also yield ideas for the starting point in the process of building.

Often we will discover that the needed change has its roots in another area altogether. I remember God speaking to me about a change I needed to begin based on Philippians 2:19-21: "I hope in the Lord Jesus to send Timothy to you soon, that I also may be cheered when I receive news about you. I have no one else like him, who takes a genuine interest in your welfare. For everyone looks out for his own interests, not those of Jesus Christ."

I needed to work on meeting the needs of others even when doing so was consistently inconvenient for me. So I devised a plan that involved looking at some verses about serving, and also scheduling opportunities to direct myself to other's specific needs even though the times were not convenient for me. When I found myself angry as I carried out this plan, I realized that I wasn't dealing with the root of the needed change— my selfishness! I shifted my strategy to dealing with *that* area and God began to change me.[1]

Recognizing at least some of the roots of an issue helps us aim our efforts at the real need. Perhaps that means we'll begin our battle with a sinful habit where it starts—at the temptation level. Or we'll tackle a contributing attitude or restructure the belief that habit is based on to line up with God's truth. We may begin a new process of maturing by starting to practice one of its contributing characteristics.

A wise plan begins with understanding and action at the root level.

2. *What are its fruits?* When sin or negative

habits are involved, the fruits may be blatant or hidden, but in either case they are destructive. Who is affected by this pattern or attitude? How has it altered our relationships? How tangled up are we in its complications? What results of this do we actually like? What principles does God give that relate to this area?

Facing honest answers will produce a myriad of ideas for growing in understanding of God's perspective, and for beginning to correct some of the negative results of our present condition in this area.

When the issue is one of growth and development, what results should we be looking for? How can this change process be demonstrated in our lives now? Who will be affected? What patterns or habits can we form to support this new growth? What does God say about progress in this area?

As we think through such questions, we'll discover areas for study and opportunities for action. We can plan to begin demonstrating the change we are trusting God to make, just as Gideon moved out against the Midianites confident of victory. James calls this "faith and . . . actions . . . working together" (James 2:22).

From the results of these lines of thinking we can develop a plan, made up of a series of steps, to enact obedience. A wise plan will aim at increased understanding and specific practice. There is no one "right" plan. If we are careful, thoughtful, prayerful, specific, and focused on God's design in the area in which He has spoken to us about obedience, God will Himself use the series of steps we have planned. He will unleash His power within us in a way that far exceeds our meager resources, our limited understanding, and our personal abilities.

Both the as-we-go obedience that takes and makes daily opportunities to live out God's Word, and the longer process that requires more thought and planning are essential to the race of obedience. For the runner, this is like developing his strength and ability, while at the same time also remembering to eat properly, tie his shoelaces snugly, and dodge obstacles in his running path. If either the daily care or extended training is missing, the running is severely hampered.

In the race of obedience, both the as-we-go applications and the longer processes are part of our love expression to God. I find that I can work on only a small number of longer processes at a time (some involve weeks, some much longer), but can be continually aware of obeying God as I go.

Regardless of whether our step of obedience is singular, or the first one of a longer plan, there are some principles that will be helpful as we plan and act.

1. *Be dependent on God.* Remember, our efforts are not the source of change. *God* is. Just as driving onto the conveyor is our part at the automatic car wash, so understanding and action are our part in seeing God change and use our lives. In neither case does our involvement achieve the end result, but in both cases it makes the result possible. This blend of God's part and our part is aptly

expressed in Isaiah 26:12: "All that we have accomplished you have done for us."

Pray for God to correct and develop the area He has you working on. Ask for His perspective and acknowledge your willingness to hear and act. Praise Him for all He will do.

2. *Use reminders.* The wilderness of Israel was dotted with piles of rocks. Men of God had created these reminders when He spoke or acted and the people needed to remember what He had said or done. To all who passed by, the piles of rocks were memory-joggers of God's Person, work, and words.

Reminders are a valuable help when we're working on correction and progress. A sign on the desk, or over the sink—"Use kind words."—can catch the critical tongue. A watch alarm set to go off hourly can remind its wearer to pray briefly, developing a habit of unceasing prayer. An index card used as a Bible bookmark and bearing the question How can I carry out this truth? can encourage the reader to plan steps of obedience. A certain landmark passed daily can trigger a response to commit our situation at work, at home, or at school to God.

Use reminders generously, helping to ensure that "you do not forget the LORD your God, failing to observe his commands" (Deuteronomy 8:11).

3. *Remember the replacement principle.* Ephesians 4:22-24 describes this principle: "You were taught, with regard to your former way of life, to put off your old self, which is being corrupted by its deceitful desires; to be made new in the attitude

of your minds; and to put on the new self, created to be like God in true righteousness and holiness."

If we plan to *replace* ungodly habits, thoughts, actions, and attitudes with godly ones, we'll discover it's far more effective than merely attempting to make the old ways disappear. For instance, replacing an angry response with a soft answer is far more effective than simply biting our tongue.

4. *Be accountable.* For a longer plan, have "checkups." A note to yourself on the calendar, a friend recruited to help, or an open and honest Bible study group are all helpful ways to stay accountable. Are you carrying out your plan? What's the next step? What is God doing in this area?

Accountability also involves getting help: "Do you have any books on this? I'm trying to change in that area of my life." Or "Hey, if you hear me complain, will you give me a pinch?" When we get others involved, it automatically keeps us more accountable than when we attempt our obedience in isolation: "As iron sharpens iron, so one man sharpens another" (Proverbs 27:17).

5. *Be diligent.* It is easy to lose heart when we come face to face with our own stubbornness. In most areas that need significant change or development, we will make progress slowly. After all, we've been that way a long time! If we take the long view, rather than anticipating overnight success, we'll find it easier to stick with it. Diligence is essential in this race of obedience: "The plans of the diligent lead to profit" (Proverbs 21:5).

6. *Be encouraged!* God has big plans for little

steps! He has always intended that His Word be lived out in the character and conduct of His people. As we carry out our love for Him with our willing understanding and obedient action, we will be fulfilling His desire and ours, to "love the Lord your God with all your *heart* and with all your *soul* and with all your *mind* and with all your *strength*" (Mark 12:30, italics mine).

Notes

1. I highly recommend Larry Crabb's book, *Effective Biblical Counseling* (Zondervan, 1979), for a biblical understanding of the underlying issues of sinful patterns.

9
The Road Ahead: Pressing On in Strength

The young servant boy's eyes sparkled with excitement as he darted into the house to deliver the news to Timothy. Usually polite, today he abandoned his manners and exploded into the room where Timothy sat engrossed in discussion with several young men. "Hurry, Master Timothy! Come quickly! The gate! A man at the gate says he has a letter from Master Paul!"

The boy eagerly searched his master's face for the transformation he had come to expect when news of any sort arrived from the beloved Paul. A joyful, understanding look passed between them, and Timothy squeezed his young friend's shoulder. "Let's go!"

The two of them hurried out to the gate,

where a messenger from Paul was waiting for them, a young man whose life had also been deeply influenced by the aging and imprisoned apostle. Stifling his longing to read Paul's words, Timothy patiently inquired about the young man's journey, a few of their common friends, and Paul's health. Soon the servant boy was preparing a meal and a quiet place for the weary traveler to rest.

The group of young men at Timothy's table got up as he came back to the house; they understood the significance of a message from Paul. Graciously leaving Timothy alone to read his letter, they knew he would freely share Paul's words with them when the time was right.

By himself at last, Timothy sought the quiet of his long, narrow room, where he sat on a ledge by the window in the end wall. Timothy's hands trembled as he opened the letter. He realized that the last hands to touch the inside of this letter were Paul's. Immediately a picture flashed into Timothy's mind: Paul in the chilly semi-darkness of a stone-cold Roman prison, chained to guards, unable to get comfortable as he composed his letter.

Timothy brought the parchment to his nose and thought he could smell the mustiness of the prison cell. How he longed to comfort Paul, to wrap a blanket around him, to pray with him, to encourage him with the news of growing believers! He had so many questions, too, and could almost hear Paul saying, "Let's talk, my son," as he had said to Timothy countless times in the past.

But Paul was over a thousand miles away, and

Timothy knew that he might never hear Paul's voice again. Perhaps this letter was the last communication he would ever receive from Paul. The significance of this probability clutched at his heart, and he realized that Paul must have had the same awareness. If so, he held in his hands the spiritual last will and testament of a man whose obedience to Christ had affected not only his own life, but also the lives of many thousands of people.

With this solemn realization in mind, Timothy began to read: "Paul, an apostle of Christ Jesus by the will of God, according to the promise of life that is in Christ Jesus, to Timothy, my dear son: Grace, mercy and peace from God the Father and Christ Jesus our Lord" (2 Timothy 1:1-2). *What a God-filled man*, Timothy thought. *Even as he suffers, he focuses on the promise of life and expresses such tenderness!*

Several lines later he came upon some words confirming his suspicion that Paul knew the end was near: "What you heard from me, keep as the pattern of sound teaching, with faith and love in Christ Jesus. Guard the good deposit that was entrusted to you—guard it with the help of the Holy Spirit who lives in us" (2 Timothy 1:13-14).

Tears blurred Timothy's vision as he grasped the import of Paul's words. He had repeatedly illustrated the life of faith as a long-distance race that required long-distance obedience. Now reaching the end of his race, Paul was passing the torch to Timothy, whose own striving for the goal still stretched ahead.

After finishing the letter, Timothy began

reading it again, eager to let Paul's challenge strike deep within him. Paul was finishing his race in the grace and strength of God, and he wanted his beloved Timothy to run and finish equally well. In his first letter, Paul had placed the responsibility of a holy life squarely on Timothy's shoulders: "Train yourself to be godly" (1 Timothy 4:7). Amid his detailed instruction concerning church administration, worship, special circumstances, and problem situations, Paul had also given Timothy a bigger vision. He knew that Timothy could get so bogged down with the details of living that the larger picture could easily fade into obscurity. He had to help Timothy look clearly at God's eternal purpose and see the details of obedience in the greater context of the life of faith.

+   +   +

Timothy's need is also ours. As we anticipate the steps of our race yet to be run, we need to remember the larger context we must develop as we live out our obedience. By our choices we can create life patterns that match up to God's purpose—habits based upon biblical priorities. Such a context encourages and assists our daily efforts to obey God as He directs us in specific situations. Without it, our efforts to obey can become isolated incidents, devoid of relationship to the rest of our life. If we run the race this way, we have little chance of finishing well.

The larger context Paul was writing about to Timothy is spiritual fitness. A physically fit person has a far greater ability than a physically unfit person to respond consistently to physical challenge. Similarly, spiritual fitness empowers us for more consistently obedient responses to God in the challenges of life. But unlike physical training, the effects of spiritual fitness are far-reaching and all-inclusive, as we can see in Paul's emphasis to Timothy: "For physical training is of some value, but godliness has value for all things, holding promise for both the present life and the life to come" (1 Timothy 4:8).

In his final letter to Timothy, Paul provided several crucial insights into how to develop the spiritual fitness necessary for the long-distance race of obedience.

God's purpose

Paul reminded Timothy that God has called us to a holy life "because of his own purpose and grace" (2 Timothy 1:9). Our growth in holy living is God's purpose for us individually (that we know, serve, and become like Him) and as His Body, the church (that we represent God in the world as we grow up in Christ and draw others to Him). Paul had given his life for God's purpose, and he knew that Timothy's heartbeat echoed his own. Paul had even testified to the Philippians that while others looked after only their own interests, Timothy attended to the interests of Jesus Christ.

Yet Paul still needed to remind Timothy of this high calling, this life of ultimate and eternal purpose. Why? Because it is easy to lose sight of our calling in Christ. Even as we take steps of obedience at each opportunity, we can forget the goal of our call to holiness and the focus of our goal, our Lord Jesus Christ. With this short-sighted vision, we become disheartened. A fading purpose makes today's challenge hardly worth the effort. Enthusiasm gives way to weariness.

What is the way out of this descent into spiritual depression? Lift your eyes, says the writer of Hebrews (12:2). Put your focus back on Jesus and His call and purpose in redeeming you, "so that you will not grow weary and lose heart" (Hebrews 12:3).

When we again grasp the fact that our God, the Creator and Sustainer of the universe, the Author of redemption, the Supreme Ruler, has called us to holy living as a worthy expression of our love for Him and our partnership in His Kingdom, the daily challenges take on new meaning. Today's steps are significant strides in "the race marked out for us" (Hebrews 12:1). We *are* fulfilling God's purpose.

God's priorities

When Timothy had finished reading through Paul's intense and straightforward letter, he was clearer about his priorities than ever before: *Be faithful to God. Be faithful to the responsibilities God has given me.*

Paul's entire letter to Timothy was directed at these two priorities. As Timothy lived out his faithfulness to God and his God-given responsibilities, he would be fulfilling his call to a holy life. Paul urged him to "continue in what you have learned and have become convinced of" (2 Timothy

3:14). Perhaps Timothy was reminded of Paul's caution in his first letter: "Timothy, my son, I give you this instruction in keeping with the prophecies once made about you, so that by following them you may fight the good fight, holding on to faith and a good conscience. Some have rejected these and so have shipwrecked their faith" (1 Timothy 1:18-19).

Our priorities as Christians are identical to Timothy's. From teenager to aging great-grandparent, from pastor to politician, from new believer to seasoned follower of God, we who are Christians share these two all-encompassing priorities: Be faithful to God; Be faithful to what God has entrusted to our responsibility. Our daily obedience will inevitably fall under one of these priorities, placing our current steps of application within the framework of the eternal purpose of God.

Each of us has many life components to place in priority—for example, family, job, church, ministry outreach, leisure time, friendships, routine duties, finances, and personal development. Books, Bible studies, and seminars abound on the topic of how to organize these priorities. Most of us have given some thought to what our priorities are. The difficult task is knowing how to order them to live faithfully in the ever-changing dynamics of life.

I recently had occasion to ponder this issue of priorities in an unlikely setting: sitting in my dentist's chair, studying a mobile that hangs from the ceiling. The mobile is made up of several colored balls. The largest one hangs directly beneath the ceiling hook, and the rest of the configuration stems from, and is held together by, that one large sphere. Below it, threads and long steel wires hold smaller balls of different sizes and colors in balanced relationship to one another. If the air in the room is relatively still, those balls remain stable in their relationship. When something disturbs the air, the balls dance and bob, constantly changing position relative to one another until the disturbance is over and they settle back into balanced form.

Watching the movement of this mobile, it struck me that if we try to keep our priorities entirely fixed, we'll become frustrated with the normal as well as the exceptional demands of life. Our relationship with God should remain our unchanging first priority. The rest of our priorities are subordinate to that relationship, and fall into balance with one another according to their relative importance. This balance gives us a basis for choosing between priorities, making time commitments, and so forth.

From time to time, urgent needs and shifting circumstances send gusts across our mobile of priorities, temporarily changing the balance of their relationships to each other. A career change, for example, may for a time keep a parent busy on evenings usually devoted to the family. A death throws everything into turmoil, as do weddings and births. When these gusts subside, our priorities can return to their former balance. That return will be much quicker and clearer if we have developed patterns and habits that reflect our chosen priorities.

Patterns and habits

Understanding our God-given priorities is one issue; structuring our lives to reflect those priorities is quite another.

Our manner of living always reflects certain priorities. How we handle time, money, relationships, responsibilities, and choices reveals more about what is actually important to us than any list of priorities we might come up with. We might claim that our relationship with God is our first priority, but unless our life shows some evidence of its primary importance—for example, consistent choices of opportunities to know and obey God and His Word—we are in reality living according to some other top priority.

Paul knew that patterns based on God's priorities help to develop the spiritual fitness essential for the long race of obedience. These patterns strengthen and condition us for the race ahead. In his first letter to Timothy, Paul had urged his disciple to "guard" what had been entrusted to his care (1 Timothy 6:20). In his last letter, he repeated the concern: "Guard the good deposit" (2 Timothy 1:14). Paul was strongly urging Timothy to maintain a pattern of teaching and living that would keep him on track with God's purpose and priorities.

If we do not develop patterns by choice, we will develop them by default. Paul had mentioned to Timothy in his first letter that young widows should remarry, because in their culture, without specific commitments, they easily developed "the habit of being idle and . . . gossips" (1 Timothy 5:13). Habits form according to our natural tendencies when we neglect to choose and pursue alternate patterns. *Most patterns of default detract from, rather than contribute to, priority living.*

Timothy knew that everywhere Paul had gone he had taught the believers to establish godly patterns: patterns in fellowship with their Lord, in fellowship with each other, in reaching out to a lost and hurting world, in family life, in church life, in conducting business, in treating strangers kindly, in financial matters—in every area of life. These were not to be mere cultural norms, adopted as part of a Christian lifestyle, but deliberate habits developed from God's priorities, with the conviction that such patterns contributed strength and form to the one who desired to finish his or her race of obedience well.

How can we pursue these godly patterns? How can we shape our lives around God's priorities? Godly patterns must be established consciously—by choice, one step at a time.

Time is an element we must invest in establishing these strengthening patterns. A daily encounter with God in His Word and conversations with Him in prayer are ways of living out the priority of our faithfulness to Him. Blocks of time guarded for rest, holidays, study, thoughtful conversations with friends and loved ones, and development of a skill or hobby are also deliberate efforts to reflect priorities in our schedules. Regular, honest "family councils" could be a wise time investment for many households in establishing patterns that reflect the priority of family relationships.

Deliberate scheduling is important, for these patterns never evolve on their own. Sometimes it's a genuine battle to establish and protect them—one day at a time, one week at a time. A calendar or date book can be of invaluable assistance.

After deciding to build his relationship with our two young sons, my husband began a pattern of meeting each boy for lunch once a week. If he didn't have that commitment marked on his calendar, he might frequently forget (although both boys remember these "dates" very well!) and end up with a hit-or-miss effort at best.

In addition to carefully scheduling our time, *long-range choices* are another element in setting life patterns to match God's priorities. Joshua commanded the people of Israel to "choose for yourselves this day whom you will serve" (Joshua 24:15). We often create our own obstacles in priority living because we resist making inclusive choices. Such long-range choices were the essence of Paul's exhortation to the Ephesians when he wrote,

> You were taught, with regard to your former way of life, to put off your old self, which is being corrupted by its deceitful desires; to be made new in the attitude of your minds; and to put on the new self, created to be like God in true righteousness and holiness. (Ephesians 4:22-24)

Timothy had observed that many of the believers at Ephesus had set aside their "right to vote" on issues of their former lives; they were obedient, instead. They had made the far-reaching choices necessary to "put off" the former ways and "put on the new self." Of course, their choices still needed to be worked out in the specifics of daily life, and daily application was not effortless. But those choices did provide at least two strong advantages: 1) the launch of a definite pattern; and 2) a new perspective on other aspects of life.

Picture a man who has allowed poor habits to erode his health. He has formed his patterns by default: eating too much, exercising too little, and filling his wine glass too often. Now his doctor tells him that the pain in his chest and the high numbers on his blood pressure chart are warning him to make his health a priority. The man has a choice to make—a long-range choice with far-reaching implications: stay in his let-it-happen mode and just try a little harder to "watch it," or commit himself to a new course that will reverse his deteriorating condition.

He decides to commit himself to the priority of his health, and his choice launches a new life pattern. He now sees the contents of his refrigerator, the commercials on television, and the urgings of his friends in a new light. The bottles in the liquor cabinet are no longer his friends, even though they still beckon. Walking the dog becomes an opportunity rather than a chore. The man's choice has begun a pattern that will probably add not only health, but years, to his life.

We face similar choices as we consider how we will live out our priorities. Will we respond to them with hit-or-miss efforts, or will we make committed, long-range choices that launch patterns and change perspectives? If we use our power of choice to line up practically with our priorities, we infuse strength into our race of obedience. This strength is essential to spiritual fitness, and God will use it during times of crisis to help stabilize us.

Growing in spiritual fitness is a lifetime project. In addition to using our time and our choices to create patterns of godly training, we must also *be prepared to persevere.* Spiritual progress involves struggle—not only against our own natural tendency to allow patterns to form by default, but also against more sinister forces. Timothy was well aware of the truth in Paul's warning to the Ephesians: "For our struggle is not against flesh and blood, but against the rulers, against the authorities, against the powers of this dark world and against the spiritual forces of evil in the heavenly realms" (Ephesians 6:12). Paul had also urged him to "watch your life and doctrine closely. Persevere in them, because if you do, you will save both yourself and your hearers" (1 Timothy 4:16).

Timothy knew what such perseverance might involve. Now, in his final letter, Paul again reminded Timothy of the necessity of perseverance in the race of obedience:

Endure hardship with us like a good soldier of Christ Jesus. No one serving as a soldier gets

> involved in civilian affairs—he wants to please
> his commanding officer. Similarly, if anyone
> competes as an athlete, he does not receive the
> victor's crown unless he competes according to
> the rules. (2 Timothy 2:3-5)

It would not be too long before Timothy's own endurance was tested with imprisonment. Then the words of his friend, the writer of Hebrews, would have new meaning for him: "You need to persevere so that when you have done the will of God, you will receive what he has promised" (Hebrews 10:36).

The patterns and habits we form to live out God's priorities are our spiritual fitness, our individual training in godliness. As we apply time, choice, and perseverance to establishing these patterns, we set the stage for the long race ahead. Our godly patterns will keep us on track, while our steps of obedience will help us move forward.

When he wrote his beloved Timothy for the last time, Paul was nearing the finish line of his race. He was passing the torch to Timothy only after having shown him how to run the long stretch. As Timothy thought back over all that Paul had taught him, he knew that he was prepared to endure, prepared to complete the race in faithfulness to God and the tasks God had given him. Deep within himself he knew that he, like Paul, would someday hold out the torch to another spiritual runner with the same testimony as Paul: "I have fought the good fight, I have finished the race, I have kept the faith" (2 Timothy 4:7).

10
Bondage or Freedom?
The Discipline
of Living in
God's Context

Eve is thinking. Although she is vaguely aware of
the fruit-laden trees all around her, the focus of
her gaze is a branch of the tree just in front of her.
Sunlight reflects off several of its dark shiny
leaves. The bough is arched from the weight of its
fruit. Eve is close enough to smell the ripened
sweetness.

"Well?" A voice breaks into her private
reflection. A question is waiting to be answered.

"Well, yes and no," Eve answers. "We may
eat from the trees in the garden"—Eve chooses
her words carefully—"but God *did* say 'You must
not eat fruit from the tree that is in the middle of
the garden, and you must not touch it, or you will
die.'"

Eve is still thoughtful, still staring at the tree before her. Until this moment, she hasn't really thought about this tree. She and Adam, delightfully free, have been enjoying each hour's new experiences. It hasn't occurred to either of them to question anything. When God has walked with them in the garden, He, too, seems to have delighted in their freedom, and they have all enjoyed the pleasure of being with one another. So this reflection is new for Eve, this questioning of what God has said.

She and Adam have never spoken of the one restriction God has placed on them—so insignificant compared to the vast freedom that is theirs. Now, however, it doesn't seem insignificant at all. Eve is suddenly uncomfortable, but she doesn't know why. Before she can reason with herself, the voice again interrupts her thoughts.

"You won't die!" the serpent insists. "God knows that when you eat of that tree, your eyes will be opened, and you will be like God, knowing good and evil."

Could this really be true? The forbidden tree certainly looks very attractive. Is God keeping something special from her and Adam? Is it unreasonable of God to put limits on their freedom? Does He secretly intend to keep Adam and her ignorant?

The thoughts come all at once, and Eve is hardly conscious of them. She looks at the serpent, then at the tree. Nothing seems as important right now as finding out what this fruit has to offer. Hesitating for only a moment, Eve reaches out and loosens the two closest pieces of fruit.

+   +   +

God had placed Adam and Eve in a paradise, making them co-regents over creation. They lacked nothing: they had work to do, food to eat, the constant companionship of God and of one another, and the opportunity to bring forth a family, all at the express desire of their Creator. They had complete and glorious freedom, with only one simple exception.

God designed this restriction to protect their freedom. And He told them so. If they kept themselves within the context God had set, they would protect their lives. If they did not discipline themselves to live within God's context, they could expect death, not as punishment but as consequence.

It seems so obvious to *us*, looking back over countless centuries, that Eve should gladly have lived within God's context. But it wasn't obvious to her. *We* can see that the real issue was God's word against the serpent's word, but Eve didn't stop to evaluate the implications of challenging God's word. Neither did Adam. Instead, they allowed both their reasoning and their feelings to tell them that a lie was the truth and the truth was a lie. In doing so, they lost the freedom they thought they were seeking, and gained the bondage they thought they were escaping.

It is clear that to obey God requires the exercise of personal discipline. Self-discipline is necessary in listening, understanding, praying, planning, and choosing consistent application. Practical commitment stands or falls on the issue of our willingness to control our will.

Disciplining ourselves wisely is never easy, however. No formula exists for making self-control an automatic response. From now until we die, we'll face the challenge of wise self-discipline: "Therefore, brothers, we have an obligation—but it is not to the sinful nature, to live according to it. For if you live according to the sinful nature, you will die; but if by the Spirit you put to death the misdeeds of the body, you will live" (Romans 8:12-13).

While it will never be easy, such wise self-discipline is a significant tool that God has provided in calling us to walk worthy of Him. And He has put it well within reach. "Therefore," Peter says, "prepare your minds for action; be self-controlled" (1 Peter 1:13). Unfortunately, because we often don't understand what God means by this personal discipline, we can make the effort, even the *idea*, of self-discipline excruciatingly painful.

Some time ago, the topic of self-discipline came up unexpectedly in the midst of a discussion I was involved in. The sudden introduction of this topic produced noticeable physical responses among those in our group. Several people bristled defensively as tension replaced enjoyment of our conversation. Others slumped slightly in their chairs. One person piped up with the suggestion that self-discipline was simply a matter of total surrender to God. Some disagreed, arguing that although they were committed, they felt they just couldn't "juggle all the balls" successfully enough to keep life unified. To them, this meant that they weren't self-disciplined enough.

What a disheartening thought these individuals labored under! Is the aim of self-discipline to "get it all together" and keep it that way? If so, then certainly most of us are fighting a losing battle. Reality just won't fit into such an ideal; things fall apart with annoying regularity.

Such thinking leads to bondage, and, in a sense, to death. Some of us remain perpetually sad because we have finally faced the fact that we can't juggle it all; we think we have failed. Self-discipline has become a forbidding high-jump bar, and no matter how hard we try, we just can't get over it. Our hearts are heavy with self-incrimination, and we feel we have disappointed God. Enthusiasm, zest for living, creativity, and even hope have all died in the attempt. We feel relegated to the sidelines, out of the race.

But *God's* purpose for self-discipline intends exactly the opposite effect: our liberation from such self-imposed bondage. How we have mis-shapen this tool of God, that we perceive it as an impossible standard! In our perception of God's commands as restrictions rather than gateways to freedom, we fall prey to the same lie that captured our ancestors in their garden paradise.

What is wise self-discipline?
Part of the lie we believe is that God is hemming us in at every turn, and therefore we can't possibly

keep ourselves within all those limits at the same time. It can feel like trying to keep a dozen Ping-Pong balls under water; we just get one down and another pops up!

We assume that God has the same perspective of self-discipline that we do, and most current literature serves to foster this false assumption. Are we really dealing with God's idea of self-discipline when we try to fine-line every aspect of life in an attempt to make it all neat and tidy? Or are we actually just pandering to our own need to feel that we have everything in order and under control?

Wise self-discipline can be simply defined as *faithfully working to conform our lives to the precepts of God's Word in order to be more like Him as we walk through life*. Perhaps we have tightened our belt of rules and forgotten the simplicity of Micah 6:8: "He has showed you, O man, what is good. And what does the LORD require of you? To act justly and to love mercy and to walk humbly with your God."

God's context for us is amazingly vast and His limits really very few by comparison. His challenges are great, but He's designed them to be possible and enjoyable, if taken one step at a time. But we have actually added on to what God commanded, and then berated ourselves for not being able to keep up with the standard.

Eve added to God's commandment. He explicitly stated that she and Adam were not to *eat* of the tree of good and evil. When Eve repeated God's words to the serpent, she added, "And you must not touch it." That simple addition made God's simple rule (designed to protect them) seem quite unreasonable.

God is not asking us to get it all together. "He knows how we are formed, he remembers that we are dust" (Psalm 103:14). Rather, He is urging us to be careful to live within His protective, life-giving context as we run our race. And He wants us to run it one day at a time. His desire for us is abundant life and true freedom, and both of these are the consequences of disciplining ourselves under His control in the *process* of knowing and becoming like Christ.

Such understanding can free us from the unrealistic demands we make on ourselves. Paul tells us, "It is for freedom that Christ has set us free. Stand firm, then, and do not let yourselves be burdened again by a yoke of slavery" (Galatians 5:1). God wants us to stop putting ourselves in a self-made position of slavery. Then we will be able to concentrate on His simple desires for us.

Self-control still will not be easy, but we will gain new and deeper motivation for it when we see it as a tool for cooperating with God in the freedom He has designed for us. Just as man is free to fly when the machines he builds conform to aerodynamic laws, so we are free to become all God intends as we discipline ourselves according to His life-giving Word.

God is the source of personal discipline

Another aspect of the lie we tend to believe (often unconsciously) is that God has left us on our own in this area of self-control. Certainly we can *feel* alone as we struggle uphill with a particularly stubborn issue—as if God has laid down the law, given us a resource pack of verses, and is now standing back to watch how we fare. This perception will only plunge us into an overwhelming sense of helplessness, making us feel like a victim of circumstances that crash over us like angry waves.

Feelings, and the perceptions they bring, are probably the most changeable aspect of human nature—sometimes delightful, sometimes miserable, rarely dependable. Because feelings are often the strongest element in our response to our situation, we must be alert to separate them from truth. The ability to feel, and to feel strongly, is from God, but He never intended that we harness our understanding and our will to our feelings.

Rather, our feelings, although sometimes very strong, are really just followers. They follow what we actually (consciously or unconsciously) believe. I experienced this progression one Saturday morning not too long ago, when I woke up with an unaccountable sense of heaviness in my spirit, a "black cloud" over my head. When I remembered that my feelings follow what I believe, I began to ask myself what I was believing about the day ahead.

Brian, my husband, had already left for an all-day commitment, I had a toothache, two of my three children had invited friends over for the day, and I could hear rain pelting the windows. It wasn't too hard to figure out what I believed about the day: it was going to be horrible—an endurance test at best and a disaster at worst! I also believed that such a day would push me to my limit, perhaps even past it.

Once I acknowledged what I believed, I could see that although the facts were real, my conclusions were a lie. The day was *not* doomed to disaster; God would develop *perseverance*, not helplessness, through the experience; and the indwelling Christ could and would strengthen me to endure, be patient in, and benefit from whatever might happen. I began to look up verses that clearly spelled out these truths. Interestingly, as I determined to believe the truth, my black cloud lifted and my feelings changed.

The serpent wanted Eve to harness her feelings and perceptions to a lie. He never openly challenged her to disobey God; instead, he countered God's truth with a lie, knowing that if Eve began to believe the lie, her feelings would follow and she would act on what she believed and felt was true.

If we *feel* alone in controlling ourselves, helpless in exercising our wills, victimized by people or situations more powerful than we are, we need to separate these feelings from what is true. The truth is, of course, that we are not alone in the battle of personal discipline. Not only is God present with us, He Himself is the source of any true exercise of godly discipline. Paul says in 2 Timothy 1:7, "For God did not give us a spirit of timidity, but a spirit of power, of love and of self-discipline." The word translated "self-discipline" in the *New International Version* and "a sound mind" in the *King James Version* is from the root word *wise*. It carries the sense of a sober control that results from wisdom. This is the spirit God has given us. It is beyond willpower, beyond New Year's resolutions. It is different from mere drive and determination. It is a *supernatural gift* from our loving God to propel us forward in godliness.

When we are able to use self-control as we train ourselves in godliness, it is because God enables us. When we line up our will with the truth of God (instead of with a lie or with our feelings), and when we choose to discipline ourselves based on that truth (whether or not our feelings are supportive), we are living out the power of God. It may seem to us that our determination or our strong convictions or our sheer willpower have enabled us to imitate God. But although we must contribute to self-controlled living, we must also realize that it is God who even makes that possible, and who goes so far as "to will and to act according to his good purpose" within us (Philippians 2:13).

As we increasingly understand self-discipline in the context of God's enablement to live according to the truth, we begin to obey God with a new freedom, because He is setting us free—from the bondage of lies, from inappropriate subjection to feelings and desires, from the sense that He is asking too much. Jesus promised this freedom in John 8:32: "Then you will know the truth, and the truth will set you free."

We are, and can increasingly become, liberated to focus on God and His good intentions for us. Such liberation releases within us the joy of the race, and we can run with renewed vigor, calling out to God, as David did, "I run in the path of your commands, for you have set my heart free" (Psalm 119:32).

With this perspective of God's work in our lives, the plain hard work of personal discipline no longer looms as impossible. Most of us don't mind, and even enjoy, working hard when we really want the end result. We may fall on our face and get discouraged, but we get up and keep going. Gradually the discipline pays off, and we begin to harvest the fruit of our hard work. Musicians, researchers, students, dieters, and anyone else who is motivated to reach a goal has experienced this process. It's part of life, this persevering discipline for a purpose. If we maintain our motivation for that purpose, we keep getting closer and closer to our goal.

The real difficulty in maintaining personal discipline lies not in the effort, but in our motivation. This element is the key to exercising God's gift of self-discipline as we live within His context. Eve lost her motivation when she stopped believing the truth that freedom, fullness of life, and fellowship with God exist only within His limits.

God desires and plans incredible Christlikeness for our lives. His limits outline the context in which we can know and become like Christ. As we work hard to live out the truth of God's Word, using the spirit of self-discipline that He has given us, we can be profoundly motivated to run this exalted race of freedom that God calls obedience.

11
In the Battlefield: Fight the Good Fight

The television commentator was attempting to help his listening audience grasp the impact that on-the-spot photography had made on Western society's perception of war. Before cameras were introduced to the battlefield, he explained, almost everyone who lived far from the war zone held a romantic and idealized view of war. Fighting men were dispatched amid much fanfare and glory and were welcomed home in the same manner. Those who returned often brought exciting tales of battle heroics and usually wore their wounds proudly as badges of loyalty. Those who never came back were frequently pictured as having died a hero's death, loyal to the end, meeting their Maker in a blaze of glory.

Battlefield photography ripped through those notions, however, tearing away every vestige of idealism about war. Even in black and white, these pictures portrayed such unheard-of horrors that almost overnight the Western nations began to recoil from what they had previously so eagerly embraced. Hard realism made soldiering a matter of sober commitment rather than naive pride. Those who did go to war left home shores better prepared and far more solemn than their forefathers had been. This new awareness seeped through every strata of society, altering our whole approach to armed conflict. For the Western world, war had lost its romantic glamor.

As Christians, we must discard any romantic notions we may have about *spiritual* warfare. It is neither ethereal or glorious. It is not distant battles fought by missionaries in foreign lands. It is here, right now. You and I are in enemy territory. Our race of obedience is run on a battlefield. We can be sure that spiritual advance will be met by opposition.

Life isn't easy for *anyone*. But everyone who moves out in obedience to God will find that the battle becomes fiercer. For as followers of Christ, we experience more than the common struggles of human existence. We actually do battle with the forces of evil, and we wage war against sin and its effects in our own lives. It is this sometimes outward, sometimes inward battle that Paul refers to when he asserts, "For our struggle is not against flesh and blood, but against the rulers, against the authorities, against the powers of this dark world and against the spiritual forces of evil in the heavenly realms" (Ephesians 6:12).

God has not sent us onto the battlefield as naive recruits, wistfully hoping for the best. *We wage war as conquerors.* The battle is real, but the victory is just as real: "In all these things we are more than conquerors through him who loved us" (Romans 8:37). There is no battle, inward or outward, in which we are not already victors. To face the brutal reality of the conflict with the confident skill of a conqueror—that is our battle call.

Enemy tactics

He sat shivering and hungry. Wilderness stretched in every direction, leaving him alone and vulnerable. The gray sky threatened rain again. Already the ground was muddy, choked with leaves that had fallen in the force of last night's downpour.

Suddenly another figure appeared on the bleak landscape. The Tempter had arrived to challenge Jesus to battle. Arrogant, he observed the weak and bedraggled Man who stood to face him. He finally had Jesus where he wanted Him, and he could almost taste the sweetness of victory.

His first attack was cruel: "If you are the Son of God, tell these stones to become bread." The Tempter's aim was pointed: get the Man to focus on His excruciating need, and challenge Him to deal with it now, using the means offered. The two stared into each other's eyes. Without unlocking His gaze, Jesus answered the Tempter: "It is written: 'Man does not live on bread alone, but on every word that comes from the mouth of God.'"

Slightly wounded, the Tempter launched his second attack: "If you are the Son of God, throw yourself down. For it is written: 'He will command his angels concerning you, and they will lift you up in their hands, so that you will not strike your foot against a stone.'"

In the long pause that followed, Jesus thought about the Tempter's words. He was being challenged, in effect, to tell God how and when to prove Himself. Jesus' answer was clear: "It is also written: 'Do not put the Lord your God to the test.'"

Desperate now, the Tempter became more direct. He offered Jesus the lordship of the world, there and then, if Jesus would worship him. He would not have to go the route of the Cross; it would be quick and simple this way.

Jesus' answer came swift and loud: "Away from me, Satan! For it is written: 'Worship the Lord your God, and serve him only.'"

For a brief moment Jesus was alone again; the Devil had disappeared as suddenly as he had come. Then, in a wave of relief, Jesus welcomed His Father's angels, who arrived to minister to Him in His need.

+   +   +

In Matthew 4, God has given us a picture of the stark reality of spiritual conflict. As it was for Jesus, so it will be for us. The Tempter *will* attack. The issues *will* be real. The temptation *will* be strong.

But Jesus is the genuine Victor. He is a Conqueror who knows the heat of battle. We have only a few "photographs" of His combat experience, but we know that no attack of the Enemy is foreign to our Christ: "For we do not have a high priest who is unable to sympathize with our weaknesses, but we have one who has been tempted in every way, just as we are—yet was without sin" (Hebrews 4:15).

The Evil One is no less aggressive in his ploys against our lives. He blends deception and a detailed knowledge of our weaknesses to attack us where we are most likely to fall. Sometimes the attack will be direct, like a hand grenade exploding in our face. Joseph experienced such an overt attack when Potiphar's lustful wife tried to force him into her bed. Job suffered one direct hit after another as he plunged into a trench of illness, death, and destruction.

The effect of such an attack is not only to offer a strong temptation, but also to allow the surprise effect to throw us off balance. Then, in our panic, we grab at straws, and turn away from trusting God.

Even events that don't originate with Satan become tools he uses to try to pull our focus off God. And not all the tools appear to be negative. Although we are certainly vulnerable during difficult times, we are equally vulnerable at times of success. Whether we lose a job or get promoted, we are open to shifting our gaze (and our dependency) from God to ourselves.

We need to be keenly aware that Satan will try to arrange or use any circumstance to draw our focus away from God. With practice, we can train ourselves to recognize Satan's direct attacks. They usually originate in outward circumstances, and often we face a distinct choice of whether we will trust God or go another route.

Far more subtle, however, is the Enemy's tactic of providing the option of a wrong means to meet a legitimate need. His attacks on Jesus took this form. It was legitimate for Jesus to be hungry, to want God to intervene miraculously in His life, and to want to exercise His lordship over the world. All these desires originated in God's design. But Satan's solutions did not, and it was the *solutions*, not the *needs*, that Jesus attacked when He countered Satan's onslaught with God's Word.

We live in a consciously need-centered age. We spend multiple millions of dollars on determining our needs, and even more dollars on trying to meet them. We talk about, think about, plan around, and are often consumed by, our needs. This context is a ripe opportunity for Satan to offer counterfeit answers. *All* of Satan's solutions are counterfeit; *all* his promises are lies.

God will show us how our needs are to be met in *His* way. Sometimes our needs will even have to be placed on hold while God deals with something in our life that He considers more crucial. Our point of understanding these things is God's Word. If we do not know the Scriptures, we will be easily duped.

The enemy will not only attempt to shift our focus off God, and tempt us to meet our needs his way, but he'll also work to get us sidetracked.

Satan's lying whispers suggest that God is not to be trusted. If we listen to them, we grow fearful.

Joshua, it seemed, constantly fought fearfulness. God continually encouraged Him to put aside his fear: "No one will be able to stand up against you all the days of your life. As I was with Moses, so I will be with you; I will never leave you or forsake you" (Joshua 1:5). Had Joshua doubted God's assurance to him, he would most likely have aborted his mission of leading the Israelites into the Promised Land.

Busyness is another tool Satan will use to sidetrack us. He convinces us that every need is a demand and that our lives are filled to overflowing with "have-to's." Martha of Bethany faced this issue because of a mealtime when Jesus and His disciples were staying at her home (Luke 10:38-42). Moses faced it when the whole burden of decision-making for his people rested on his shoulders (Exodus 18:13-27). The apostles faced it when the administration of the rapidly growing church began to usurp the time and energy they should have been investing in the ministry to which God had called them (Acts 6:1-7). Many obligations may well be legitimate, but when they outgrow their bounds and distract us from the very purpose they serve, we are sidetracked.

A third means of distraction that the enemy uses is what I call "tunnel vision." We become consumed with our own perspective, our own projects, our own aims. These may well have originated in our commitment to Christ. But somewhere along the way, we have narrowed our sights so that we no longer see our efforts as part of the whole picture of what God is doing in the world and in His Church. We become enamored with our role. Our perspective narrows, our concerns turn inward, and our resources are consumed on keeping it all going. We arrive at a point, even in the midst of all our "spiritual" labor, where we are looking out for our "own interests, not those of Jesus Christ" (Philippians 2:21).

Satan will use any means available to preoccupy and sidetrack us. Money, relationships, causes, negative attitudes, and several dozen other factors could be added to his list of tools. If he can maneuver something into the position of dominance in our lives, he has succeeded in sidetracking us from a single-minded love of God.

Our enemy's aim is to destroy us. His efforts blend easily into the kaleidoscope of life and may not seem so harmful. But that is part of his deception. His ways are deadly; he is a murderer (John 8:44). And so Peter sternly warns us, "Be self-controlled and alert. Your enemy the devil prowls around like a roaring lion looking for someone to devour" (1 Peter 5:8).

As we take steps of obedience, our enemy is waiting. He *will* engage us in battle. He may attack directly, and wrestle with our focus. He may ambush us, deceiving us into meeting our needs with his means. Or he may infiltrate our lives little by little, diverting us from a clear and single-minded devotion to Christ.

Our only appropriate response is prepared resistance: "Submit yourselves, then, to God.

Resist the devil, and he will flee from you. Come near to God and he will come near to you" (James 4:7-8). That resistance is to be founded in God's truth and enacted with His resources (see Ephesians 6). Our awareness of the enemy's strategy, and our readiness to resist based on God's truth, will help us to stand in the battle. We should pray that in spiritual warfare, as Jesus desired, we will "be as shrewd as snakes and as innocent as doves" (Matthew 10:16).

Internal battles

The more we set our eyes on God and place our footsteps in His ways, the more acutely we will know the reality of our own inner battle with sin. We will find a kindred spirit in Paul as he agonizes over his struggle with sin:

> For what I do is not the good I want to do; no, the evil I do not want to do—this I keep on doing. Now if I do what I do not want to do, it is no longer I who do it, but it is sin living in me that does it. So I find this law at work: When I want to do good, evil is right there with me. For in my inner being I delight in God's law; but I see another law at work in the members of my body, waging war against the law of my mind and making me a prisoner of the law of sin at work within my members. What a wretched man I am! Who will rescue me from this body of death? (Romans 7:19-24)

Hebrews 12:1 tells us that God knows how

easily sin entangles us. It is our penchant to sin that leaves us open to temptation. If we are honest, we must acknowledge that our skillfulness at sinning and our ability to deceive ourselves are frightening realities in spiritual warfare.

We are told not to sin. As we grow in awareness of what God says and in specific obedience to His Word, we'll often be dealing directly with our own sin and its consequences. As we plan our obedience in dependence on God and develop life patterns that strengthen us in this battle, we will move forward.

But sometimes, instead of moving forward, we end up moving backward; we sin. Deliberately or caught off guard, we cross the limits God has set for our lives and protection, and for His honor.

How do we deal with our failure to obey? Often we respond with discouragement and depression. A fatalistic, "What's-the-use?" attitude creeps in to undermine our commitment and our momentum. Sometimes it seems as if we fail and sin more often than we succeed and obey. Then it's hard to avoid wanting to give up.

Compounding our discouragement, we become self-accusing. In the wake of a legitimate failure to obey, even honest mistakes loom as personal condemnations. While we wallow in the "Why-can't-I-make-this-work?" frame of mind, we pick ourselves apart, and cloud an even larger part of our perspective. We begin to feel like a burden to God, and we seem to feel His divine disappointment fall heavily upon our shoulders.

If we have genuinely repented before God of

specific sin, then what we actually are sensing is not God's disappointment, but a weight of our own making. And that weight hinders our race (Hebrews 12:1). Without diminishing the seriousness of sin, let us look for a moment at God's perspective of our race of obedience.

God created man to fellowship with Him. Sin ruined that fellowship, but God has taken the initiative to draw us back to Him—culminating in the incarnation, death, and resurrection of Jesus. God's desire for us was so powerful that He willingly offered Himself in exchange for our lives. And His love is so unimaginably great that even our outright rejection will not stop Him from pursuing our response.

In the light of such love, and by the power of such grace, we have come to Him and now stand before Him. He is profoundly pleased with our desire to love and obey Him. He desires our fellowship. He yearns for our joy. He works on behalf of our needs and desires. He draws our eyes back to Him when we look away. He awes us with Himself. He disciplines us in love when we persist in straying outside His life-giving limits, because He sees the harm we are doing. He transforms our lives to conform to His original design.

In this framework of the love and grace of God, we sometimes rebel, and often fail. Have we done irreversible damage to the pleasure God takes in us? Absolutely not! We may incur more of His discipline, and certainly we grieve Him, but we do not change His desire toward us.

We can never reduce God's resources to

cleanse and power to restore. Christ secured our forgiveness and redemption at the Cross. His work there cannot be altered. Even as we were dependent on Jesus' merits for our salvation, so we are dependent on them for our daily forgiveness and healing. Paul says it well in Romans 5:1-2:

> Therefore, since we have been justified through faith, we have peace with God through our Lord Jesus Christ, through whom we have gained access by faith into this grace in which we now stand.

Nor can we change God's commitment to His purpose in our lives: to conform us to the likeness of Jesus Christ. This is *His* work. And He has insured, in Christ, that someday it will be complete.

In the meantime, we battle Satan and sin, and even though we are conquerors in Christ, we often allow ourselves to be defeated. But as we look to God for His forgiveness, we see not an angry Lord, but a loving Father. His arms are open wide, just as were those of the father in Jesus' parable, whose wayward son had finally dragged his humiliated self home. Jesus is not keeping count of our failures. His attention, unlike ours, is focused on the fact that we turn to Him, and in this He delights:

> Therefore, there is now no condemnation for those who are in Christ Jesus, because through Christ Jesus the law of the Spirit of life set me free from the law of sin and death. (Romans 8:1-2)

The accusations that go on after we have sinned and then come to God in repentance are not from God. They are lies and must be countered with the truth. Such an understanding might seem to make light of sin, but in fact, it has the opposite effect. As we sense the deep love of God, His unending pleasure in the fact that we are His children, and His eagerness to make us more like Jesus, we find a more powerful force at work in us as we seek to be obedient.

That force is the love and grace of God. And the nature of God's love and grace causes us to want more seriously to please the One who is already pleased with us. We are more able to press on after falling and repenting, therefore, because we begin to focus (as God does), not on the wrong we have done, but on the unlimited ability we have, in Christ, to keep on pleasing Him.

This is what God did when He set us free from having the outcome of the battle resting on our shoulders. He set us free to fight valiantly, not to count our defeats. He set us free to respond to His love, not merely His judgment, because Jesus bore that judgment for us. He set us free to obey, in the thick of the battle, simply because we please Him.

Sin and Satan have no real hold on us. The only thing they hold is death. Although we do battle with the hand of death at every turn, we are alive in Christ and we stand in the grace of God. And it is God's love, grace, and power that make spiritual warfare move toward ultimate victory.

As we soberly engage in combat, assured of

the love and power of God, and trusting in *His* perspective of the battle, the psalmist's words will be true of us:

> It was not by their sword that they won the land, nor did their arm bring them victory; it was your right hand, your arm, and the light of your face, for you loved them. (Psalm 44:3)

12
Take a Step Now

Peter glanced at the man in the boat. This is actually rather humorous, he thought—conducting a teaching session from this smelly craft! But it was obvious the Teacher didn't mind, and so Peter was glad to be of service. Actually, he was more than glad; he was proud. People came for miles to hear Jesus, and would have given anything to get as close to Him as Peter was now. Content in these circumstances, he listened carefully to Jesus, his hands mending nets by memory.

Soon Jesus dismissed the crowd and turned His attention to Peter. "Put out into deep water, and let down the nets for a catch," He said.

This Man may be a great Teacher, Peter thought, but He doesn't know much about fishing. And it's the wrong time of day to be learning.

"Master, we've worked hard all night and haven't caught anything," Peter replied. Yet something about Jesus suddenly made His instruction seem reasonable. "But because you say so, I will let down the nets."

Luke 5:6-11 records for us what happened when Peter did as Jesus commanded:

> When they had done so, they caught such a large number of fish that their nets began to break. So they signaled their partners in the other boat to come and help them, and they came and filled both boats so full that they began to sink. When Simon Peter saw this, he fell at Jesus' knees and said, "Go away from me, Lord; I am a sinful man!" For he and all his companions were astonished at the catch of fish they had taken, and so were James and John, the sons of Zebedee, Simon's partners. Then Jesus said to Simon, "Don't be afraid; from now on you will catch men." So they pulled their boats up on shore, left everything and followed him.

+   +   +

This passage shows us at least three major results of Peter's obedience. First, he experienced Jesus' power, unleashed as soon as he obeyed. Jesus manifested His divine ability in terms Peter could understand: an astonishingly large catch of fish, beyond the bounds of Peter's imagination.

Second, Peter clearly saw Jesus, and he got a good glimpse of himself by contrast. This new knowledge, and the grip it placed on his heart, dropped him to his knees: "Go away from me, Lord; I am a sinful man!" Jesus had shown not only His power to Peter, but also Himself. This vision plunged Peter into a broken state, from which he could utter only desperate words acknowledging his sin and powerlessness.

Third, Peter decided to leave everything and follow Jesus. From now on, he would do whatever Jesus said. Peter had a small glimpse into the life to which Jesus was calling him. Now he wanted nothing less than a life of obedience to his Lord.

The response that Jesus seeks from us is the same one He sought from Peter: doing what He says because He is our Lord. This obedience must come, as did Peter's, in the matters at hand, in the things of which our lives are made. We must push on through the thinking and the planning into the doing.

Jesus had many more far-reaching things to do in Peter's life than stun him with a miraculous load of fish. Within four years, this fisherman would himself "catch" thousands of men, bringing them into the Kingdom of God. Peter would so know the power of God at work in him that he would confidently assert, "His divine power has given us everything we need for life and godliness through our knowledge of him who called us by his own glory and goodness" (2 Peter 1:3). And his intimacy with his Lord would give him a keen understanding of God's faithful response to His obedient children: "Humble yourselves, therefore, under God's mighty hand, that he may lift you up in due time. Cast all your anxiety on him because he cares for you" (1 Peter 5:6-7).

Peter obeyed Jesus in a fishing boat. He went on to obey Him wherever they went—on the road, on a mountainside, in a household. Sometimes he failed, and that was no surprise to Jesus. But increasingly, he lived as Jesus wanted him to live. And Jesus took the obedience Peter offered, drew him close to Himself, changed him, and ultimately used him to set spiritual fire to the world. Without that obedience, such a life would have remained a dream.

Peter's obedience brought with it a humble brokenness—a brokenness that reflects the painful awareness of how far we are from the design God intends. But God uses this awareness to lead us, as He did Peter, into a closer relationship with Him:

> The LORD is close to the brokenhearted and saves those who are crushed in spirit. (Psalm 34:18)

Just as Peter's obedience began in his boat, so our path of obedience begins right where we live, with the issues and choices that make up our lives today. What effort of obedience will you and I make this day? What opportunity is at hand? What will be our first step in living the commands of God? "Do not merely listen to the word, and so deceive yourselves. Do what it says" (James 1:22).

Jesus' words in John 14:15 go straight to the heart of the matter:

If you love me, you will obey what I command.

Let us love God today with our obedience. He asks us to let down our nets because He wants to change our lives. He will draw us close to Himself, impact our worlds through us, and make us like Him. For His glory. For our freedom.

Starting now.